£10

GW00493131

Philosophy of
Meaning and Representation

Philosophy of
Meaning and Representation

R.C. Pradhan

D.K. Printworld (P) Ltd.
NEW DELHI-110015

Cataloging in Publication Data — DK

Pradhan, R.C. (Ramesh Chandra), 1950-
    Philosophy of meaning and representation.
    Includes bibliographical references (p.   ).
    Includes index.

    1. Meaning (philosophy). 2. Representation
(philosophy). 3. Philosophy. I. Title.

ISBN 81-246-0069-4

First Published in India in 1996

© R.C. Pradhan

Published and printed by :
D.K. Printworld (P) Ltd.
Regd. office : '*Sri Kunj*', F-52, Bali Nagar
New Delhi - 110015
Phone: (011) 546-6019; *Fax* (011) 546-5926

Dedicated to
my
Eldest Brother

Preface

THIS book is an attempt towards presenting a representational theory of linguistic meaning. The framework for understanding meaning presupposed in this theory is the representational theory of language. By representation here is meant the linguistic representation which philosophy of language in general deals with. These representations are different from, and independent of, the mental representations which constitute the subject-matter of the cognitive sciences. Mental representations are so-called because of their functional-computational character and their ability to be represented in a formal computational machine. They are, however, states of the mind or the brain which is understood to be of the character of a complex machine. Linguistic representations, on the other hand, are logico-grammatical structures which are capable of being analysed formally. These structures are syntactically and semantically analysable and are thus open to grammatical systematization. Besides, these grammatical structures are the representations of the world around us. They become the repository of meaning because of their being the representations of the world.

The present attempt is to link meaning with the linguistic representations in an effort to explain meaning as essentially representational in character. Meaning, in fact, is the essence of the linguistic structures that represent the world. It is the internal phenomenon to the linguistic representations. The birth of meaning therefore is the birth of linguistic representations as such. This presupposes that language is logically representational and cannot be conceived except as the structures that are involved in the process of representing the world.

There are two senses in which language can be defined as a set of representations. They are (a) the sense in which language is about the world, directly or indirectly, and (b) the sense in which language represents itself. In sense (a) language speaks about the world, or it is directed towards the world. It is because of this that we can say that language is the representation of the world. It is not a representation in the narrow sense that it is a description of the world, for there are non-descriptive representations as well, as evidenced in the natural languages. The non-descriptive uses of language are varied and many but, for that matter, they do not cease to be about the world. It is their **aboutness** regarding the world that makes them the representations of the world. Hence the fundamental and all-comprehensive character of the linguistic representations. In the sense (b), however, language is supposed to talk about itself in that we teach and learn language in language itself. This is a logical truth about language that it is capable of formulating its own grammatical structures such that we need not represent the latter in any other medium than the language itself. However, it must be noted that, even while talking about itself, language is keeping its relation with the world intact. There is no way of escaping the fact that language is the representation of the world in a primary sense.

The central argument of this book is that meaning is representational, since it can neither be pre-representational nor post-representational so far as it remains the fact that meaning arises only when the linguistic representations of the world take place. That is to say that language acquires meaning only by virtue of being about the world. The concept of being-about-the-world is a pre-logical concept and therefore precedes the logical analysis of language. Language and the world are built into each other; they constitute a single reality: **language-and-the-world**.

Meaning is the essence of this reality. The linguistic representations of the world reveal the fact that the world is what it is because of its being represented in language.

The theory of meaning proposed here is committed to the fact that the linguistic representations are so constituted that they incorporate the basic idea of saying something about the world in their very structure. Hence the importance of the idea of language-being-about-the world. Meaning theories in general have this conception in their background though only a few articulate it. The Frege-Wittgensteinian semantic tradition is fully committed to the idea of representation since, for it, language is logically related to the world. For both Frege and Wittgenstein, language analysis is based on the idea that language is the mirror of the world. The post-Wittgensteinian semanticists like Davidson and Dummett have veered round to the view that language is basically a system of representations. It is immaterial whether the representations are understood in terms of truth-conditions or the assertion-conditions. In either case the demand is that language be about the world and be the representation of the latter.

The crucial point is whether language can be shown to be non-representational at all as it has been claimed by the anti-representationalists like Rorty who take the inspiration from the later Wittgenstein, Heidegger and Dewey for their claim that language is not the mirror of the world. This idea that language is not representational has quite often been pressed for as the rejection of the classical theory of truth and meaning. This book addresses itself to that question and tries to argue that the notion of representation is a pre-theoretical notion and so it is independent of the debate between the realists and anti-realists over whether truth and meaning can be classically understood. I have argued that the choice is not between language as **representation** and language as **play** or **game** in the later Wittgensteinian sense, but whether we can think of language that is not about the world at all. So the basic presupposition of semantics is that language is involved in the world. This I call a representational relation between language and the world.

Language is largely a **field** in which the representations of the world take place. It takes care of the various activities that take place in language. That is to say that nothing of language is excluded from the linguistic field. In the broad sense, all linguistic activities are representations irrespective of whether they are descriptions of the world or not. So the concept of truth is not the only key to the understanding of the representations though it indirectly is. It is rather the concept of meaning that broaches the concept of representation, since in the very structure of representation itself the structure of meaning is displayed. The question of truth arises because the concept of truth is logically linked with the concept of language-being-about-the-world. But the concept of representation precedes the concept of truth as the former is logically primary. In this sense, meaning precedes truth, though they co-exist in the field of language itself.

The realist-antirealist dilemma as to whether meaning is primary or whether it is truth-dependent is misplaced for the reason that there is no conflict between truth and meaning. The field theory of language does take care of the fact that representations are the primary datum of language and so it accommodates not only the linguistic representations that are true or false but also those which are directly neither true nor false. The language that is truth-based is as much representational as the language that is not, and so there is no conflict between the so-called truth-conditions and the assertion-conditions of the linguistic representations. The truth-based semantics must take note of the human interests — beliefs and intentions — as much as the semantics of use and conventions. In that respect, there is nothing to choose between meaning as truth-conditions and meaning as the justification-conditions since both are equally rooted in the semantic space of language-use involving linguistic representations.

My solution of the problem is that realism with a human face is possible if the conflict between impersonal truth and the human beliefs and intentions is resolved. The resolution does not entail that there is no universal truth that is objective, nor does it entail that the human interests cancel the objectivity of truth. In a holistic framework, both truth and the human world co-exist. Language being inherently about the world, realism is inevitable and so is representationalism. That is the reason why meaning must make room for truth which is at once impersonal and also linked to the human world. Meaning balances the objectivity of truth with the human interests. It need not be anti-repersentational to do this balancing act as representationality alone can guarantee objectivity of both truth and meaning.

In chapter 1, I have put the realist-antirealist dilemma in a straightforwardly semantic framework. That is what I have called the semantics of representations. I have argued that the Fregean concept of sense promises to provide the foundation for the semantics of representations as in it alone we find the clue to the understanding of the relation between language and the world. In chapters 2 and 3, I have undertaken a critical study of the theory of representation in Frege, Wittgenstein, Davidson and Dummett to show that contemporary philosophical semantics has taken the concept of representation as the basic concept. I have argued that the Fregean as well as post-Fregean semantics is largely representational and so the logical relation between language and the world is taken for granted.

In chapter 4, I have been engaged with the concept of truth and its relation to the world-order. I have argued that truth is a disclosure concept in that it discloses the structure of the world. It is, in that sense, not a correspondence nor is it a pragmatic construction. Truth as such is a fundamental notion because it is primary so far as our understanding of the structure of the world is concerned. However, it presupposes that meaning of the linguistic representations has already prepared the ground for the disclosure of the world by disclosing the structure of language. Meaning therefore is no less a disclosure of the language and the world-order or the being.

In chapter 5, I have come back to the problem of meaning to show that meaning and representations are internally linked and that meaning is representational as much as language is. In this lies the fact that meaning is the primary datum of language and so must be considered the key to the understanding of language and the world. That is the reason why the realist cannot claim that meaning is truth-dependent, nor can the antirealist claim that truth is not relevant to meaning. In fact both meaning and truth are co-present in the dynamics of the linguistic representations since language is basically about the world. Language is the mode or the form of our being in the world and therefore there is no escape from being linguistically involved in the world.

In chapter 6, I have argued that semantics is an autonomous discipline and that it cannot be reduced either to a natural science of human behaviour or to a cognitive psychology. I have argued especially against Quine's naturalism by showing that meaning is not a matter of behaviour and that there are facts of the matter in semantics that cannot be reduced to natural facts. So semantic facts are autonomous and need a non-naturalistic treatment. In this context, I have argued that what Quine calls the first philosophy cannot be abolished as long as meaning refuses to be a product of the natural events and processes. Meaning transcends the natural world of facts being a normative reality and so is open to a transcendental validation. Hence the possibility of non-natural grammar of meaning and truth is still open.

My argument in this book can broadly be called transcendental in the Kantian sense in that I have argued that meaning is possible and that there are constitutive conditions of this possibility. I have shown that naturalism in the theory of meaning leads to scepticism and so we must opt for a theory that takes language and meaning as autonomous. The theory of representation argued for in this book promises to fulfil the twin theses of representationality and autonomy of meaning.

The bulk of the material which constitutes this book was written at Oxford while I was a Commonwealth Academic Staff Fellow at the University of Oxford during 1990-91. It took almost four years or so to systematize it into the present form. Though I am not happy even with this form, I felt that unless I bring them into certain order now I will never be able to do it. I do not claim finality about any of the claims made here and I feel that no such claim can ever be made in philosophy.

The book is rather short and is very brief on many points. I have mentioned many important theories only passingly and have not attempted to elaborate them either because they are not my main concern or because they are too familiar in the literature. I have developed the theme of representation and meaning and so have confined myself to the concepts relevant for this exercise. Many theories of meaning available have not been touched at all precisely for the above reason.

I have had the privilege of working with Professor Dummett for three terms at Oxford and I had the opportunity of discussing many of the issues presented here for long hours with him. I am grateful to him for giving me time for these discussions and the encouragement to think afresh on the problems. I am also grateful to many other philosophers with whom I had either brief or prolonged discussions during my stay at Oxford. Amongst them I must include Professor Hilary Putnam who visited Oxford and St. Andrews at that time, Professor Crispin Wright who delivered special lectures at Oxford, Professor Millikan who was a visiting philosopher then at Oxford, Professor Peacocke, Professor Swinburne, Dr. Hacker and Dr. Dan Isaacson, all at Oxford. These encounters with the creative thinkers has helped me to think on my own even if imperfectly. I owe a debt of gratitude to them for their inspiration.

My collegues in the Department have been very encouraging and helpful. I am grateful to Professor Suresh Chandra and Professor Ramamurthy for their advice and encouragement. I am thankful to Dr. Amitabh Das Gupta, Dr. Chinmoy Goswami, Dr. Raghuram Raju, Dr. S.G. Kulkarni, Dr. K.S. Prasad and Mr. Anand Wazarwal for their ungrudging help and friendly co-operation.

I am thankful to the authorities of the University of Hyderabad for granting study leave to undertake the project of post-doctoral studies under the Commonwealth Fellowship Programme. I am thankful to the British Council for their help and cooperation. I am thankful to the Department of Philosophy, Oxford University for providing me all the facilities in the library for my study.

I am grateful to the Co-ordinator, DRS Scheme, Professor A. Ramamurty and to the Vice-Chancellor, Professor G. Mehta for the substantial grant released for the publication of the book.

My wife, Jhansi and my sons, Nachiketa and Sabyasachi have been very patient with me during my long absence from home. Without their love and care I could not have done the work. I owe a special debt of gratitude to them. I also express my gratitude my eldest brother, B.B. Pradhan for his encouragement and to all my family members for their help and inspiration.

Lastly, I am thankful to Sri Susheel K. Mittal, Director, D.K. Printworld (P) Ltd., New Delhi for undertaking the publication of the book.

Hyderabad

1996   **R.C. Pradhan**

Contents

Contents

1

Foundations of a Theory of Meaning

UNDERSTANDING of meaning is, broadly speaking, the understanding of language. Therefore the understanding of the foundations of a meaning theory must lie in how we develop the theory of the structure of language. Language and meaning belong to the same logical space as do logic and logical form. Hence the investigation of one leads to the investigation of the other. When we understand language we understand its structure, organization and above all its meaning. Thus the syntax of language goes collateral with its semantics.

Semantics is traditionally assigned the task of investigating meaning while syntax is the study of the linguistic structure and rules. However, the investigation of meaning presupposes that language has a syntactic structure which must be displayed in a rule-structure grammar.[1] Meaning is the collateral phenomenon that accompanies the structure of language. The structure of language brings out the meaning when it is suitably interpreted and thus meaning and structure of language are interdependently embedded in the same logical space. Meaning is the expression of thought which language expresses in its logical structure.

Frege,[2] for the first time, made us aware that meaning or sense is involved in the logical structure of language, since, according to him, language is the primary vehicle of thought and that the logical form of language expresses the logical form of thought. Sense, according to him, is the thought that is expressed in the logical structure of language. Frege made the logical syntax and semantics the study of sense, the former studying the logical structure of the vehicle of sense, i.e., language and the latter its interpretation in the domain of external objects, that is, the world. Semantics thus inevitably brings in the notion of reference as the method of interpretation of the syntactic structure. Hence arises Frege's famous distinction between sense and reference[3] as the foundation of logical semantics.

Frege's semantics of sense can be considered the foundation of a theory of meaning that proclaims adherence to the concept of meaning as the expression of thought in relation to the world. The latter concept can be characterized as the representational concept of meaning. The concept of linguistic representation is a significant notion in contemporary logical semantics as it has been the central notion for understanding the concepts of truth and meaning.[4] Wittgenstein's *Tractatus* has very eminently made the concept of representation the logical basis of understanding of language and meaning. Both Frege's sense (*sinn*) and Wittgenstein's representations have been the most significant concepts of logical semantics.

The representational semantics that is proposed by Frege and Wittgenstein has made meaning a matter of logical representation of the world. It proposes a representational line between language, thought and the world. In this way it draws the boundary of the semantic space which articulates the structure of language as well as the structure of meaning. The following is the nature of the semantic space that coherently builds up the semantic line:

Semantic space: Language→ Thought→ World.

This model of meaning differs from the triangular model that represents meaning in the following way:

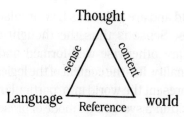

This model does not integrate all the components into a single space as the notion of representation is missing. The gap between sense and content and between sense and reference remains wide open such that no single space of meaning emerges. The representational model fills up the gap.

Semantics of Representations

The notion of semantic space introduced earlier stands for the totality of the semantic constituents of what we have called linguistic representations. The representations are, as already indicated, linear and unidirectional and thus have two constant poles, namely, (a) the pole of logicality and (b) the pole of worldliness. The pole of logicality stands for the logico-linguisticality of a symbol or the symbol-system and the pole of worldliness stands for the consummation of the symbol as a representational medium. The unidirectionality of representation consists in linking language with world via the interpretation of the linguistic categories which we shall call thought. Thus thought is included in the semantic space as the interpretation of the linguistic categories. The linguistic representations are semantically sensitive to the interpretation of the linguistic categories in a world-directed way. Thus there is unity in the semantic space, that is, a sort of holistic asymmetry that unifies sense with content and sense-content with reference. The semantic space is asymmetrical and yet synchronous, since sense, content and reference occur simultaneously, though asymmetrically.

Frege's theory of sense is the bedrock of the semantics of representations being outlined here. Frege situated sense at the core of language,[5] that is, as the essence of the sentences which are about the world and are judged as true or false depending on what the world is. Sense is thus the thought-content of the sentences which are otherwise well-formed and are compact with representationality. It is the content of the logically structured sentences that represent the world in a particular way, that is, represent the world in a systematic mode of presentation. Frege defines sense as the mode of presentation of the world such that it contains the method and the criteria of representing the world rightly or wrongly. Thus the onus of the Fregean semantics lies in the way the world is represented rather than in the world itself. In it, besides, lies the possibility of truth and falsity of the sentences themselves, though Frege, unfortunately, called truth and falsity the referents of sentences.[6]

Frege was interested in the sentences and their logical function in language. This led him to the theory that the sentences must be anchored in the world such that they could be either true or false. The semantic categories of truth and falsity are the fundamental ones so far as the semantic assessment of the sentences is concerned. This can be done if and only if the sentences are representations of the world. So Frege makes it the fundamental principle of his semantic theory that sentences must have sense in their capacity of being representations of the world. There is a logical link between sense which is the representational thought embedded in the sentences and the truth-conditions that semantically follow from the sentences being the representations of the world. The link between sense and the truth-conditions is a purely logical or internal one, since sense logically determines the conditions of the truth and falsity of the sentences. The sentences are true or false by being the expressions of thought about the world and thus there is an internal mechanism by which those thoughts are to be assessed to be so. This is possible only if there is already a criterion available in language for the assessment. According to Frege, sense provides this criterion in the form of the norms of judging whether the sentences are the right representations or the wrong ones. Frege's sense would have been a fragile notion had it not been the logical ground of the assessment of the representations of the world. Sense saves the representations from being only contingently applicable to the world. The idea is that sense is the inherent feature of language that imposes on the world the capacity to respond to the sentences.

The Fregean framework thus does open the possibility of the logical link between thought (sense), language and the world. The relation between thought and language is considered to be so logical that there is no room for making it possible that thought can be non-linguistic. Frege certainly does not intend to make thought completely independent of language, though he concedes that sense is independent of the natural languages it being out and out a logical entity. The latter concession is not against the idea that thought is logical in its structure. The relation between language and the world is equally a matter of logical relation such that the structure of language goes a long a way in fixing the structure of the world. Thus the structure of sense is crucial to the understanding of language and the world.

Frege is the founder of representational semantics as he has realized that in this semantics alone there is the possibility of locating sense in language itself. Though sense itself is a logical entity it needs the linguistic medium to express itself and therefore there is the enormous importance of language as the medium or vehicle of sense. Representational semantics hinges on the idea of language expressing thought such that there is an immediate need to relate language to the world. The language-world relationship is the bedrock of the representational relations signified by sense. Sense is the seat-anchor of these relationships such that once we grasp the structure of sense we can grasp the language-world relationships in a transparent way.

Frege's sense is partly logical and so normative, and partly ontological. Logically speaking, sense is a pure entity locked up in the world of logic and therefore has a normative existence so far as its semantic application is concerned. But, in addition to this, it has an ontological existence such that it is real as a semantic entity. Frege argues that without its ontological reality sense cannot be the normative principle of semantic assessment of the sentences. There is therefore a happy union of the normative semantics of sense and its ontology as it is only as an objective reality that sense can be the foundation of the truth-conditional semantics.

Frege's semantics is based on the principle that sense is cognitively available in that it can be grasped by the mind in all its details. However, it is not primarily an epistemological notion as it does not bring in the structure of consciousness for its identification. It is graspable, nonetheless, in the consciousness and can thus belong to the cognitive repertoire of the mind. But that does not constitute the nature of sense. Sense is above and beyond the domain of consciousness. It is in any case mirrored in the medium of language and thus its linguistic availability is guaranteed. This ensures that sense being ontologically real does not go against its being available to the linguistic understanding.

The semantics of sense, however, does not solve the problem as to how sense, being a real entity in the ontological sense, can be expressed in the linguistic medium which is supposed to be contingent in the world. The linguistic medium being primarily a medium of expression of sense or thought, it could be the case that thought remains independent of language and goes completely unexpressed. Frege admits that there is no way sense or thought could be made language-dependent so long as language, in the ordinary sense, is highly ambiguous and so unfit for being an effective medium of sense. In this sense language is highly contingent and so cannot express the sense which is necessary and autonomous.

Wittgenstein could sense the real difficulty in Frege's semantics and opted for a stronger role of language in the representational framework Frege developed. It is language and language alone which in the *Tractatus* plays the role of cementing the gap between language and thought. Thought is completely mirrored in language since both have identical logical structures and both are in the same logical space. That is, the logical form of language is the same as the logical form of thought. In view of this, Wittgenstein could argue that there is no danger of thought or sense being unrepresented in language and that sense is fully a language-dependent entity. This avoids the other danger of language being contingent and so being unfit to express thought transparently.

This leads Wittgenstein to propound what is known as the theory of autonomy of language which establishes that language is already there before we could begin to understand thought or sense. So sense itself must be language-dependent and in that sense no semantic interpretation is possible in the absence of language. The fundamentality of language is evident in the fact that language is the home of thought or sense. This also introduces the idea that thought itself is logically a representation of the world in that the world has the same structure as language and thought. Wittgenstein echoes Frege'concern for the language-world relationship but makes it not an ontological issue at all. He solves the so-called ontological issue on the logical plane by showing that thought and language together make up the logical space that makes the notion of world-representation possible.

Thus the theory of world-representation becomes the crucial component of the semantics of representation both in Frege and Wittgenstein. Whereas in Frege semantics is still concerned with the problem of sense and reference and how sense can determine the reference in the world, Wittgenstein goes a step further in telling that neither sense nor reference is sufficient in itself to fix the relation between language and the world. So, for him, there is no semantic problem of settling the language-world relationship. The relationship is built into the semantic space that takes care of the sense and reference of the linguistic representations. There is an effort in Wittgenstein to overcome the semantic dualism between sense and reference and to integrate them into a single frame of reference that can be called a semantic framework. This can better be called the logico-linguistic framework that generates autonomously the logical criteria of evaluating the linguistic representations of the world.

Language as a Universal Medium

Wittgenstein's semantic framework can be appreciated only if we keep in mind that for him language is a universal medium.[7] The semantics of representations does necessitate the fact that language is treated as a system of symbols that not only represents the world but also it constitutes the logical criteria of what makes the symbol-system coherent and consistent. In view of this, the following two theses may be considered for examination:

(a)   Language is the universal medium since it expresses everything relating to the world and ourselves within itself. Even our understanding of language is expressed in language without requiring a metalanguage.

(b)   Language contains its syntax and semantics, that is, it contains its grammar without presupposing an independent medium to express the rules of grammar.

The thesis (a) is generally known as the expressibility thesis[8] or the effability thesis that tells that nothing is beyond the expressive power of language. To this both Frege and Wittgenstein are committed in spite of Wittgenstein's rider to the contrary[9] that language has limits in its expressive power. But insofar as the semantic rules themselves are concerned, both Frege and Wittgenstein are aware that no metalanguage is involved in expressing them. This leaves room for the fact that the rules are shown in the very fact of their linguistic formulation. This has been characterized as an ineffability thesis by Hintikka[10] for an altogether different reason that semantics cannot be formulated in language. This, however, is not the reason to believe that there is another language than the actual one we have for fomulating it. In fact our language expresses the semantic structure within itself.

The universality thesis lays it down that not only the world-representation but also the semantic principles of representation are all expressed in language. So the thesis (b) puts it in so many words that the grammar of language which includes the syntactic and semantic rules must be a part of language. That is the reason why Frege maintained that sense and reference are semantic features of the logical language and there is no need of a higher language to express them. Frege has been very careful to note that logical language is the transparent medium of the sense of the expressions. Wittgenstein has made it the absolute basis of his integral theory of sense and reference that there is no higher language to express the grammatical features of our actual language as it is the only one available with us. This even precludes the possibility of a private idiolect to express the semantic criteria one comes to evolve to evaluate one's linguistic representations. The universality of language merges into its public character in that there is nothing worth the name to call anything as a private discourse.

Wittgenstein calls for the thesis (b) to counter the possibility that grammar can be independent of our language such that one can formulate a language of one's own. The universality thesis makes it mandatory that no language is possible if it is not able to contain its own grammar. A similar realization made Frege accept a distinction between logic as calculus and logic as language[11] such that no language is a mere set of notations and rules like a calculus which could be easily invented by people. It is, rather, a language in the sense that it expresses thought and, especially, logical thought so that language and logic become one at least so far as logic itself provides a universal language in its purest logical form. Frege called this universal logical language the *begriffsschrift* that expresses thought in the most transparent way.

Frege made a distinction between the logical language and the natural language in view of the fact that the latter fails to express the logical thoughts in a transparent way because of the inherent defects such as vagueness and ambiguity. These defects are removed in the logical language and thus it becomes the fit system to express the thoughts concerned. In this sense Frege considers the logical language the language of logic. It is not that logic is in need of a perfect language that can be artificially constructed but that the natural language itself can be improved to express the thoughts more perfectly and transparently. Frege remains a philosopher of language in spite of the fact that his interest is in how logic can be shown to be the universal domain of laws of human thought. The law-governed character of human thought necessitates a language that can perfectly, though in a regimented way, express those thoughts.[12] The Fregean idea of a universal logical language does provide the foundation for the logical semantics and makes it necessary that the logical thought is the primary desideratum that semantics must organize in its network of concepts and rules.

The semantics of the later logicians proved to be immensely indebted to Frege for the basic insight that the sense that is embedded in language must be of the character of the Platonic forms so that logic is permanently a study of logical forms which are little affected by the psychological location of these thoughts. Semantics as a study of the sense and the truth-value of the sentences must presuppose that thoughts are fully expressed in language and are the real contents of these sentences. Wittgenstein himself is indebted to Frege for this insight though he is credited to have said that the natural language itself is quite capable of expressing the thought-contents logically and perfectly. For him, the natural language is in perfect logical order[13] and therefore needs no radical change. If this idea is sound, then the Fregean semantics need not have to posit a Platonic world of sense or thought. Wittgenstein has shown that semantics must show rather than postulate the semantic rules, since the latter are already underlying the language we use.

Universal Language and Universal Grammar

The way Frege and Wittgenstein have advocated the idea of a universal language does suggest the importance of language in the human affairs. They have, very logically, brought language to the centre-stage of human life and thought. Two concepts have enriched the idea of a universal language, namely, the idea of logical structure of language and the idea of representationality of language. The first concept suggests that language must have a logical structure, that is, it must have a logical form that can be common to all languages whatsoever. The philosophical justification for such a notion lies in the fact that no language can be conceived unless there is logical syntax and semantics for it. Logical syntax shows that the rules of organization of the sentences must be grammatically formulated and the semantics lays down the rules that constitute the meaning of the sentences. Thus the notion of grammar emerges on the scene as representing the logic or the logical structure of language. The ideal of a universal grammar representing the rules of language becomes a philosophical necessity.

The second concept itself articulates the necessity of linking language to the world. This is better done by bringing in the idea of representation which suggests that language says what the world is, and depending on that, truth-value of the sentences is fixed. Thus language is considered to be a representational system that is logically built into the syntax and semantics of the language. The logical relations of sentences and their meaning and truth depend on the fact that language is the system of symbols representing the world.

The idea of the representational system is the bedrock of the recent revolution in philosophy of language and grammar. In spite of the appearances to the contrary, it is the idea of representation that dominates the syntactic and semantic studies of the present century. This is especially so in the logico-linguistic tradition initiated by Frege and Wittgenstein. The notion of grammar that has emerged in this tradition is the one that has made it mandatory to introduce the concept of rule and the rule-structure of language. This has facilitated the idea of understanding language as a logical system in that language is not a mere jumble of words and sentences and that it has an inherent structure that can be called logical. Philosophers of language do admit that the structure of language is and must be logical since there is no other structure which can be called universal and necessary. Besides, there is no guarantee that philosophy can study language without the prior notion of a logical structure at all. Thus the notion of grammar emerges to highlight the rule-structure underlying language.

Grammar can be defined as the self-conscious articulation of the rules of language and in this sense it is not an empirical phenomenon at all. Chomsky has recently made the claim that grammar, to a great extent, is an empirical theory of language such that by formulating such a theory we can map out the actual structure of a language. In this sense, it is the universal grammar[14] which is the original source of all languages and therefore is embedded in the linguistic faculty of mankind. This view of grammar is obviously different from that of the logical grammar which Frege and Wittgenstein are ready to accept. The difference lies in that the logical grammararian is not interested in the fact that grammatical rules are also empirical and that they are embedded in the human mind or brain. This, however, does not preclude the fact that grammatical rules are really universal and necessary.

Logical grammar is distinctly self-conscious in that it evolves a logical method for understanding the rules of language. Grammar, for this reason, is not unconscious in Chomsky's sense. As Tarski[15] has claimed, without a logical method the semantic structure of language cannot be studied in that the notion of truth cannot be defined, and if it is attempted, it will lead to semantic paradoxes. This approach to grammar led Tarski to develop a metatheory of grammar such that we have not only the formalized structures of object-language but also a formalized structure of the metalanguage. This ensures a paradox-free semantic system and obviously a truth-definition that applies universally to all languages partaking of the rule-structure of the logical grammar.

Tarski fulfilled the Fregean dream that there must be a universal system of logical rules that can characterize all languages which express our thoughts. Tarski's claim that such a system exists in the logical grammar goes towards making it real that no language can be capable of expressing sense that does not follow the rules of logical grammar. Tarski himself was not interested in the meaning question as he took it for granted that meaning or sense is the underlying feature of all languages. Meaning therefore is not to be analysed but must be presupposed in the semantic system. It is the concept of truth which needs a thorough probe in that it creates puzzles in the ordinary, unsystematic language. Without an explicit truth-definition the semantic system is almost incomplete. Hence Tarski's effort to offer a truth-definition that suits the grammarian's intentions.

Tarski's logical grammar, however, does fail to relate truth and meaning because in his system they fall apart. Whereas meaning is universal, truth is made provincial in that it is bound to be language-dependent, according to Tarski. Such a result follows inevitably as truth has to be defined in the context of an object-language and we have to homophonically include that language in the metalanguage itself. Thus we cannot ensure the universally of truth. This seems to be an un-Fregean result and for this Tarski's notion of metalanguage is responsible. The metalanguage has kept it open that it inherits the grammar and the ontology of the object-language and that it can accommodate the logical categories of the higher order.[16] This makes truth dependent on so many grammatical and logical presuppositions. So it becomes more and more language-dependent and ultimately a provincial ontology is needed to define it.

In Tarski's logical grammar truth becomes immanent in that it is a feature of grammar because only when we systematize grammar we encounter the concept of truth. This is different from the idea that truth is a primitive and indefinable notion as accepted by Frege and later by Wittgenstein and Davidson. The latter idea can be called a transcendental notion as it is not bound up with a particular grammatical system and is available in all systems. Though Tarski himself realizes that what he means by truth is the one ordinarily available in logic, yet while defining it he has hedged it in so many ways that he cannot but find that truth has become a much restricted concept.

In the present context, it is necessary that truth and meaning must go together since, in a representational system of language, the focus is as much on truth as on meaning. Especially in the natural language tradition, there is the demand that language be treated as the vehicle of meaning such that it is the responsibility of the grammarian to fix the conditions of meaning in the representational system itself. Both Frege and Wittgenstein have considered the representational character of meaning as the primary condition of language. In this sense it is easy to locate the genesis of representational semantics in the idea that truth and meaning must have something to do with how language is related to reality. Logical grammar, as conceived by Tarski, tells us in so many words that the truth-conditions must be well articulated to fix the meaning of the sentences.

In view of the above, it is certain that it is logical grammar alone that can claim universality as it maps out the conditions of truth for all the sentences of a language. At least Tarski attempted such a universal grammar for all languages. The only condition of such a grammar is that it is embedded in the metalanguage which may include the object-language itself. There is, however, no extra-linguistic reality for grammar in the Chomskian sense. Chomsky attempts to locate the universal grammar[17] in the mind itself such that the rule-structure is innate to the mental faculty. This has the implication that mind or brain has already contained the grammatical rules which underlie all the human languages. Such a view of grammar clashes with the idea of logical grammar which claims that the grammatical rules are ultimately linguistic in character. The latter view emphasizes that the rules of grammar are logical in character and so must be embedded in language and not in the mind. Frege himself had rightly warned that any concession to the mentalist characterization of logic will undermine the normative character of logic and logical rules since the rules of logic far outstrip the so-called empirical rules of the mentalist grammarian. In this sense the universal grammar of the empirical grammarian is less universal than the logical grammar of the logician precisely because the latter really lays down the universal or global conditions of language. That is to say, the logical grammar alone can reveal the logical structure of language even though it looks as if without empirical support it fails to locate the intended structure.

Grammar in the philosophical sense need not be constrained by the empirical details of the linguistic discovery since the structure that is taken to be true of all languages is not the result of an empirical discovery. It is the normative condition of language and not of how the language is empirically studied by the grammarian. Thus we can say that the philosophical sense of grammar is far sensitive to the internal demands of locating meaning in the structure of language which itself is concerned with the structure of the world. This is the logical condition of language that it represents the world in its logical structure.[18] The presence of the logical form of world in the inner structure of language explains how truth and meaning are possible.

Meaning and Reality

The domain of logical grammar is the domain of the necessary conditions of meaning in that grammar fixes the essence of language and the world.[19] This brings to our notice the fact that, without the essesential conditions of language being fixed, we cannot determine the conditions of meaning. As we have already seen, language is bound up with the world and so meaning must logically be related to the latter. No meaning can be studied unless and until we can tell what a sentence expresses in relation to the world. Of course the world is reflected in language and meaning is not a thing or fact which is reflected. Meaning is rather the way the fact is represented in language, or, in other words, it is the method of representing the world itself. In this sense we can say that meaning is not what is represented but is the representational content of language. Meaning is the semantic content that shows how the world is logically organized and how it is reflected in language.

The relation between meaning and the world is logical rather than factual. By understanding a sentence, for example, "The cat is on the mat" we are sure to know what the world is and also how the sentence functions grammatically in this context. It is not that meaning is another entity in addition to the function of the sentence and the rules underlying its use. Meaning is the totality of the semantic structure of the sentence. In addition, however, we are made aware of what the world is in the very structure of language and meaning. This is the connexion between meaning and reality that we are searching for. The world is, in a sense, revealed in meaning, or, if one finds this difficult to accept, one can better say that by understanding meaning we understand the world. By this we want to say that meaning is very much a concern of the grammarian and the semanticist insofar as the latter are also concerned to understand the world.

Reality, which is the ultimate object of meaning analysis, is the one we are familiar with in our everyday concerns. It is the set of properties and things that impinge on the grammatical surface in countless ways. Reality makes us conscious of the fact that we are not only the beings-in-the-world but also the beings-in-language such that all our effort to locate meaning in language directly leads us back into the world. It is so because language shrouds the world as an invisible layer and the meanings enshrined in language are concerning the world. The world can be grammatically presented in the structure of the meanings. Meaning in a sense spreads across the world constituting the latter's essence. A semantic space is constituted by the network of meanings and thus there is a two-way traffic between language and the world. Meaning is the intermediary between the passing nuances of language and the stable, though contingent, things of the world.

The world as such does not have meaning since meaning is not a contingent fact but a normative principle. The world is a system of things and their interrelationships and thus there is a nexus of causal and non-causal connexions in the world. But the semantic content called meaning does not belong to this nexus. Meaning belongs to the domain of the semantic relations amongst the words and their relations to the sentences and thus meaning is linguistic in nature unlike the things in the world. For example, a stone as a physical thing has no meaning but the word 'stone' has meaning in the nexus of other words and sentences. It is a noun-word signifying the object stone. But the word 'stone' has meaning as it occurs in the sentences either while naming it or describing it in different contexts. Apart from naming and describing, the word has other functions such as evoking wonder or expressing aesthetic joy, etc. All these are impregnated into the linguistic meaning of the word. There is no division of linguistic meaning and the non-linguistic meaning in this case since all meaning is ultimately linguistic in character. Even the so-called aesthetic meaning is nothing but the meaning accruing to a word or words which evoke aesthetic emotions. The system of meanings associated with the words and the sentences constitute a semantic space that makes it possible how the words attain a stable pattern of use. This requires the laying down of rules in the sense grammar is an essential condition of all language-use. Grammar comes into the picture as the system of rules or norms of use and thus there is a transcendence of the contingent occurrences of the words in their particular uses. The universal character of meaning emerges because of the fact that meaning is not a paticular use but the system of uses that stretch across a continuous time. The semantic potency of the word increases with the stationing of the word in the grammar. Rather, the said potency gets stabilized as the grammar is fixed for the time being.

The word and the object stand together in the grammatical nexus and there is no reason to feel that word can have meaning even when grammar does not fix the object as the referent of the word. The referent of the word is coeval with the word precisely because the word has a meaning because of the grammatical rules. The object may go out of existence and yet the word continues to be meaningful. It is because the meaning of the word is not the object itself. Grammar fixes the reference and then the word continues to function even when the referent does not exist. Thus there arises the need of the trans-temporal rules of use of the word. The rules become the timeless elements in grammar such that they make the words meaningful even when the original referents are no more existing. In this sense we can say that the life of a word outlasts the life of the objects. That is, the history of the word or for that matter, language is collateral with that of the objects but is not identical with it.

The word-object relationship is grammatically very significant. It is because the word derives its meaning from the grammatical nexus in which it occurs rather than from the world which it symbolizes. The words symbolize the world in various ways and it is not necessary that they only describe it. Description is only one of the functions of language. The symbolic function of language is diverse and multifarious. This is what Wittgenstein[20] and other ordinary language philosophers have emphasized in this century. This has gone a long way in showing that language as a symbol system is a very rich phenomenon and so needs a more comprehensive grammar. Especially, the meaning of the words and sentences must be so grammatically fixed that there is no loss of meaning for those expressions which do not fall under a fixed model. This is the post-positivist scenario in meaning analysis.

The emphasis on language and its multiple functions coincides with the realization that language and life go together. This is due to the Wittgensteinian dictum that language is a form of life[21] which has caught the imagination of the philosophers of the present century. This has led to the discovery that no meaning analysis is possible unless we situate meaning in the nexus of the linguistic activities themselves. Meaning has ceased to be a mere grammatical entity and has become synonymous with the rules meant for the regulation of the language-use. This is a radical shift in the very idea of meaning.

There is a parallelism between grammar and reality in the changed context of meaning analysis. The Fregean emphasis on the duality of sense and reference has been superseded by the theory that meaning does not depend on what the world exactly is. That is, in the present context, it is not necessary that reference must be fixed for a sentence or word to become meaningful. In fact reference is taken care of by grammar itself and so there is no independent theory of reference needed for a meaning theory. All that the meaning theory does is to relate language to the world in the grammar itself. This has become evident in the ascendancy of the sentence in grammar in the post-Fregean semantics. Wittgenstein took the lead in this respect and it has been further developed by Quine in his theory of sentence-grammar as the basic feature of language. Quine in his analysis of word-object relationship has come out with the suggestion that words are part of the sentence in their grammatical function and therefore their meaning is a part of the overall picture of language.Thus meaning-holism has led to the realization that reference is indeterminate and inscrutable.[22] The indeterminacy of reference has a further consequence so far as the meaningfulness of a sentence is concerned. Meaning can no more be fixed independently of the language-system. This Quine acknowledges to be the fate of meaning in general whatever the consequence so far as the traditional semantics is concerned. Quine's advocacy of the sentence-grammar has been partly responsible for the new understanding of the language-world relationship.

The loss of the supremacy of words in grammar does not mean that the object in the world is lost. The word fails to fix the referent in that it cannot tell what the referent is unless the whole language is fixed. This is only a semantic shift from the word-reference to the sentence that talks of reference. This can be called the semantic ascent and it is possible only when there is a total retreat to language from the world. Quine supposes that a retreat is possible so that meaning becomes a grammatical phenomenon and in the process the world is relegated to the background. This does not, however, mean that the world is lost for grammar. In fact, when the concept of truth is brought in, the world makes a quick comeback. Quine makes it clear that even when we are concerned with meaning our outward behaviour does make a contribution to the total development of meaning. For him, there is the intersubjective stimulus meaning that partly or wholly constitutes the linguistic meaning because ultimately to use language is to respond to the world in a certain way. The interaction between nature and man is fully manifest in the network of linguistic activities which Wittgenstein called language-games. Thus meaning, though independent of the world, is yet very much in the thickness of the language-world relationship.

Hilary Putnam[24] has added a new dimension to the problem of relating meaning to the world by his slogan that meaning is not in the head. This implies that meaning is not a matter of the mind but of the world. That is to say, meaning or sense is again a matter of fixing the reference of the words and therefore it depends on what the world is. Putnam is anxious to hold that meaning cannot be divorced from the public use of language and that it has to be fixed in close cooperation with the natural environment. Meaning, according to him, is a matter of social interaction in the setting of the natural world such that when we fix the meaning of a term like 'lemon' or 'tiger' we have to know what the objects are in nature. If there are no species of objects called lemon in nature there would be no reference-fixing and so no meaning-determination for that matter. What Putnam thus makes necessary for the meaning theory is that the world is veritably a partner in the business of meaning and language and so there cannot be complete indifference to the world. In fact this point is already noted and it is acknowledged by all concerned including Quine that there is no loss of the world so far as meaning is concerned. Thus we acknowledge that meaning and world are related though meaning is not dependent on the world. Meaning is grammar-embedded and in that sense reference is no more a crucial concept for meaning theory. We are not far away from the Fregean thesis that meaning determines reference though now we can say that meaning is not only that which fixes reference. Meaning is a more primitive phenomenon than reference. In this sense, it can be studied independently of how we refer to the objects in the world.

Meaning and Truth

The question of truth arises as soon as we bring in the sentences into the focus. The word-meaning as such does not raise the question of truth except indirectly. It is because the word-meanings could be entered into a dictionary while the sentence-meanings could not be done so. Sentences have to be linked with the facts in the world and so their truth or falsity has to be decided in the context of what we do in the world. Sentence-meaning requires the intervention of historical situations which results in the contextualization of the sentences themselves. The latter is the *sine qua non* of any sentence which can claim to be meaningful. Sentences are not ahistorical entities insofar as the world is being represented by them in the nexus of the grammar of a language. The fact of representation in language requires the presence of the world in its multidimensionality. Hence the historicality of the sentences in language.

The way to sentence-meaning lies through truth rather than word-reference. It is because sentences are likely to be true or false unlike the words. Sentences have the logical capacity to have the truth-values while the words do not. In this sense the sentences are bound up with the history of the world. That is, they reflect what the world is or could be provided they are made by the competent speakers. The onus of telling what the world is entirely on the sentences so that there is no other way of knowing the world except by the sentences themselves. Here lies the genesis of meaning which is what we understand when we make the sentences to represent the world. Meaning arises precisely because we are the sentence-makers and it is we who understand them. Our sentences could not be true or false unless we also understand them properly. Thus truth and meaning are co-partners in the business of the sentences. The business of the sentences is with the world and ourselves. Thus truth and meaning are the semantic features of language that engage our attention in the study of language.

However, truth and meaning are distinct semantic entities. Whereas truth is concerning the relation of language to the world, meaning is concerning the totality of the linguistic phenomena including the truth-claims themselves. So it could be maintained that meaning is prior to the truth-claims. It is semantically true that sentences must be meaningful before they could be considered true or false. This has led Frege to believe that the sense of a sentence is independent of its truth. For Frege, the truth of a sentence is the way the sense is linked with the world. The world is a partner in the fixing of the truth of a sentence whereas sense is relatively free from the world insofar as it is not a contingent feature of the world.

Following Frege, Quine has made a distinction between a theory of truth and a theory of meaning because it is the latter which gains primacy in the undersatanding of language. For Quine, meaning is a matter of language, and how we organize the language determines meaning of the sentences. Meaning is a typical human concern. But truth relates to the world in that it cancels the semantic ascent which meaning compels us to make. Thus truth is world-looking[25] and it is in truth alone that we make contact with the world. Quine's theory goes a long way towards establishing the fact that truth incorporates a significant component of reference for telling us about the world.

The question of reference is the question of making the words stand for their respective referents. This is the job of making the words signify the objects which are in the world. Thus the truth of a sentence emerges as the semantic value because of the word-object relationship. But meaning is never at stake in this reference mechanism. Meaning is presuposed in the entire process of making truth possible because of the reference of the component words of the sentences. Frege had realized the importance of reference for both words and sentences in that the world has to be brought into the picture. But sense has no such need because sense is the autonomous logical entity. Frege did not consider truth as the component of meaning or sense. Rather, truth follows sense in being the feature of the world-representation.

It is here that sentence-meaning becomes the inevitable focus of language. It is not that word-meaning is neglected but in the sentence alone the word-meaning is fully manifest. This is what the Fregean context principle[26] tells us while explaining the word-sentence relationship. The world-representation is carried out by the sentences and the sentences alone and so the words have a secondary role in the sentence. In this sense words and their references are important but, so far as meaning is concerned, the sentence has a unique role to play.

In view of the above, it is imperative that we introduce the notion of truth-conditions which are tied up with the sentences. It has been, of late, realized, notably by Davidson,[27] that meaning of a sentence is a matter of its truth-conditions. This theory does not say that meaning and truth are the same but that meaning is constituted by the truth-conditions, that is, the conditions of a sentence being true or false determines the meaning of it. Davidson's contention is that meaning is not an entity other than the truth-conditions themselves. So talk about meaning is a talk about under what conditions the sentences are true or false. This theory introduces the formal definition of truth in the Tarskian style and, basing on that, defines meaning in terms of the truth-conditions.

The concept of truth-condition is a derivative notion. It at best presupposes a strong notion of truth which itself presupposes meaning. In this sense it is not intuitively true that truth-conditions can define meaning. When we define a truth-condition in the Tarskian way following the T-schema: "S is true if and only if p", we have already presupposed meaning and in a sense have assumed that meaning is already a feature of the language in which we have laid down the truth-conditions. But the fact remains that truth-conditions are logically linked with any meaningful sentence. So Davidson is right in telling that when we approach meaning we cannot but find the truth-conditions as the logical features of the sentences. From this, however, it does not follow that meaning itself is nothing but truth-conditions.

It is obviously the case that only assertions or statements are either true or false. In that sense only these sentences can have truth-conditions. But we know that language has many other sentences which even remotely cannot be considered to be true or false. For this reason it will be difficult to define meaning in terms of truth-conditions, for it will declare that many sentences which are not assertions are not meaningful. This therefore makes it difficult to accept the truth-conditional theory of meaning as a universal theory because it does not cover all language in its purview. The representational theory of meaning considered here is ready to accommodate the notion of truth-conditions so far as it tells us that assertions are a primary source of representation of the world. Of course the non-assertive sentences are representational in a general sense. Meaning accrues to them in their representational capacity and not in their possibility of having the truth-conditions. In this sense representationality is a more primordial concept than truth-conditions. Davidson does recognize that truth itself requires a basic framework of meaning which is not always on the surface of grammar. Only by a clue given by truth-conditions to the depth-structure of semantics, meaning can be understood.

Meaning, as Davidson has emphasized, belongs to the depth-structure of language and so requires a depth analysis that takes into account the formal structure of sentences. For him, the formal structure lies in the truth-structure of the sentences. The truth-structure is the logical structure that tells how the sentential components make up the total truth-conditions of the sentence. Davidson's programme thus belongs to the formal language tradition that formalizes the meaning-relations among the constituents of the sentences. Hence the importance of the truth-conditional semantics.

Truth-conditional semantics is a continuation of the Fregean tradition in that it makes truth a fundamental concept in semantics. Frege was first to recognize that truth is the feature of sentences that cannot be further reduced to any other more primitive concept. So the notion of sense is introduced to make truth a significant concept because without sense truth cannot be placed in the semantic system. The representational semantics that we emphasize is also a semantics of sense in that it keeps sense independent of truth, though it acknowledges that truth is a feature of linguistic representations. But truth accrues to the representations only when they talk about the world directly or indirectly. It is therefore meaning which is the primary datum of the linguistic representations.

Meaning and Representations

The problem of representations is the problem of how language reflects the world. The language-world relationship is the bedrock of the linguistic representations. This has been emphasized in both the formal and natural language traditions where the focus is on how the world is logically articulated. The question of the world being articulated in language goes back to the very roots of Western philosophy wherein our thinking was considered to be a mirroring of the world. This idea has been modified throughout the centuries and the analytic philosophy has got its basic thrust from that idea. Now is the debate concerning how we represent the world in our all-pervasive language. It is in this connexion that representational semantics becomes meaningful.

Meaning is the most debatable point because, in the semantic structure of the sentences, the language-world relationship is not fully settled. The world is considered to be an alien datum to be either copied or mirrored or at best referred to But this itself is a problematic concept. So attempt has been made to make the world more internally related to language as has been done by Wittgenstein so that the question of representation does not get bogged down in scepticism. The logical gap between language and the world can be further bridged by the semantic technique of making meaning the common element between language and the world. This is to suggest that meaning which is linguistic in nature is structured into the world such that the world becomes meaningful to us because of the representational character of language.

Meaning is the semantic clothing of the world and, for that reason, it is not the contingent product of our sense-experience. The latter already presupposes that meaning belongs to the representations themselves. This is the crucial question whether we have to move beyond language to locate meaning in the contingent world of experience or we have to grant autonomy to it by fixing it in the grammatical nexus itself. There is really no 'fixing' of meaning in that sense but, so far as meaning is concerned, there is a way of locating it in the grammatical space. It is the aim of representational semantics to locate meaning in the representational system itself. This it can do by moving away from the world in search of the grammatical structure of language.

Representations are the basic ingredients of language. Whether it is the indicative sentence or a question or a command we have what Searle[28] calls the language-world fit such that in certain cases we have language-to-world fit and in other cases world-to-language fit. In any case there is a trade-off between language and the world. This makes it obligatory that the meaning of the sentences make a difference to the world. Meaning is the basic feature of all these sentences and so we find the representational content in all the sentences. This content is what Frege calls the thought-content as expressed in language.

Meaning thus brings into the fore the thought-content and its directedness to the world. The latter has been called the intentionality of language. This makes prominent the fact that there is a basic datum in language that is inalienably the representational content. This is not a psychological property of language since a mental content cannot be a semantic entity. That is why representational semantics distances itself from psychologism that perpetuates the gap between mind and language. Meaning is not a mental entity because even mental entities need a description in language. Semantically speaking, mental events and properties are equally in need of meaning as any other representation.

The need of a comprehensible theory of meaning includes the need of taking into account the mental attitudes, beliefs and the intentions of the speakers who matter to language so much. That is why the speaker's belief-system is recognizably the fundamental source of meaning. However, as we shall examine later, the beliefs do not determine meaning as they themselves need a language which is already meaningful. Those who take meaning as a collateral phenomenon along with mind are sure to miss the semantic foundations of meaning. Perhaps they have to accept that meanings are in the mind.

Representational theory of meaning assumes that meaning is not a matter of the mind. It takes the other way of accounting for meaning which can be called the semantic route. Mind for it is as much at the risk of losing meaning as any other representation unless a stronger foundation is laid down for meaning. The foundation required is in the language itself. It is the depth-level of language that reveals the meaning in its multifarious dimensions. This theory pleads for the fact that there is meaning even for the vaguest linguistic representations.

References

1. *See* Chomsky, *Rules and Representations* (Blackwell, Oxford, 1980).

2. Frege, "On Sense and Reference", in *Translations from the Philosophical Writings of Gottlob Frege*, ed. by P.T. Geach and

Max Black (Blackwell, Oxford, 1952, Reprinted, 1977), pp. 56-78.

3. *Ibid.*

4. Wittgenstein, *Tractatus Logico-Philosophicus,*tr. by D.F. Pears and B.F. McGuinness (Routledge and Kegan Paul, London, 1961).

5. Frege, *Posthumous Writings,*ed. by Hans Hermes *et al.* (Blackwell, Oxford, 1979).

6. Cf. Frege, "On Sense and Reference".

7. Wittgenstein, *Tractatus Logico-Philosophicus,* 5.511.

8. J.J. Katz, *Semantic Theory* (Harper and Row, New York, 1972).

9. Wittgenstein, *Tractatus Logico-Philosophicus,* p.3.

10. The ineffability thesis is due to Jaakko Hintikka. **See** Hintikka and Hintikka, *Investigating Wittgenstein* (Blackwell, Oxford, 1986).

11. **See** Van Heijenoort, "Logic as Calculus and Logic as Language", *Synthese* 17 (1967), pp. 324-30.

12. Cf. Frege, "On Sense and Reference".

13. Wittgenstein, *Tractatus Logico-Philosophicus,* 5.5563.

14. **See** Chomsky, *Rules and Representations* for a discussion on the nature of universal grammar.

15. Tarski, "The Concept of Truth in Formalized Languages", in *Logic, Semantics, Metamathematics* tr. by J.Woodger (Oxford University Press, Oxford, 1956).

16. *Ibid.*

17. Cf. Chomsky, *Rules and Representations.* **See also** his *Knowledge of Language* (Praeger, New York, 1986).

18. Wittgenstein, *Tractatus Logico-Philosophicus,* 4.12-4.121.

19. Wittgenstein, *Philosophical Investigations* tr. by G.E.M. Anscombe (Blackwell, Oxford, 1953) sect. 373.

20. *Ibid.*

21. *Ibid.* For a discussion on the concept of forms of life *see* my, "Wittgenstein on the Forms of Life", *JICPR* vol. XI (1994), pp. 63-79.

22. W.V. Quine, *Ontological Relativity and Other Essays* (Columbia University Press, New York, 1969).

23. Quine, *Philosophy of Logic* (Prentice-Hall Inc. Englewood Cliffs, N.J., 1970).

24. Hilary Putnam, *Meaning and the Moral Sciences*, (Routledge and Kegan Paul, London, 1978).

25. Cf. Quine, *Philosophy of Logic*, p.11.

26. Dummett, *Frege, Philosophy of Language* (Duckworth, London, 1973).

27. Cf. Davidson, "Truth and Meaning", in *Inquiries into Truth and Interpretation* (Clarendon Press, Oxford, 1984).

28. John R. Searle, *Intentionality* (Cambridge University Press, Cambridge, 1983).

2

The Structure of Representations I

In chapter 1 it was suggested that meaning is a species of representations in the semantic space. It was also suggested that the notions of meaning and representation are underlying Frege's theory of sense and Wittgenstein's picture theory of language. In this chapter I shall develop the notions of meaning and representation into a unified theory of semantics.

As indicated already, the effort here is to build up the groundwork of the semantics of representations. This requires the positing of sense as the central concept in semantics. Sense has been the central notion in Frege's and Wittgenstein's semantics for the reason that it explicates the centrality of representation in our understanding of language and the world. This is taken as the key concept in our semantic framework. But sense is no more viewed as primarily an ontological entity but as a semantic concept that carries the load of representation in language. Though Frege realized the linguistic potential of the concept of sense, he had an ontological hunch to ground it in the Platonic realm of logical entities. Wittgenstein, however, brought out this potential in the larger canvas of his theory of linguistic representations. Now is the occasion for further grounding of sense in the framework of the semantics of representations.

The semantics of representations presupposes that the linguistic representations are meaningful in the context of the world and also in the context of the total life-situations. The central concept is that language is a representation of the world. Thus meaning is objective and is rooted in the totality of language-use.

Frege on Logic and Language

Understanding Frege must begin with his conception of logic as language[1] which he believed to be the universal language containing the basic laws of thought. In the Introduction to the *Grundgesetze* Frege wrote,

> Our conception of logic is necessarily decisive for our treatment of the science of logic, and that conception in turn is connected with our understanding of the word 'true'. It will be granted by all at the outset that the laws of logic ought to be the guiding principles for thought in the attainment of truth... In one sense a law asserts what is; in the other it prescribes what ought to be. Only in the latter sense can the laws of logic be called "laws of thought": so far as they stipulate the way one ought to think.[2]

The laws of thought which are the laws of truh, "the boundary stones set in an eternal foundation which our thought can overflow but never displace",[3] are crucial to Frege's conception of logic and language. Frege wanted a universal language which transparently manifests these laws. Logic, for him, filled the bill since it itself provides a formal language of pure symbols called the *begriffsschrift*. As we have noted in chapter 1, the notion of *begriffsschrift* made a tremendous difference to Frege's conception of logic. For him, logic is not a mere calculus of deductive inference but is the domain of truth, laws and the universal language of thought. Hence Frege attached so much importance to the eternal laws prescribing the ways in which human thought and discourse have to be guided.

From Frege's conception of universal logical language the following two theses follow:

1. *The universality thesis*: logical language has a core that consists in the logical structure of sentences and their constituents. Natural languages fall short of the logical perfection of the above said language.

2. *The rationality thesis*: the method of discovering the core logical structure, i.e., the eternal laws of logic lies in reason and not in experience. Therefore logic is distinguished from psychology.

The first thesis demonstrates Frege's well-known apathy towards natural language and grammar in the study of the foundations of logic and mathematics. He does not conceal the fact that natural languages are not to be preferred to a perfect or logically adequate language consisting in pure logical notations. This he explicitly lays down in his logical treatise *Begriffsschrift*[4] outlining the main features of his logical language. Frege apparently believes that his logical language follows the model of Leibniz' *lingua characteristica*[5] which contains the rudiments of a formal language that can express thoughts logically and transparently. However, Frege does not attempt to replace or supplant the natural languages; he rather tries to improve them by adding a new notation just as we can improve the power of the eye by inventing a telescope.[6] This ought to settle the issue between logical language and its natural counterpart by bridging the gap between the two. For Frege the gap is narrow and can be overcome by increasing the logical capacity of the natural languages. Natural languages are improvable and can function well when logically regimented.

Frege's antipathy to natural languages should not be misunderstood as his antipathy to language as such in relation to thought.[7] Many philosophers believe that Frege accorded primacy to thought rather than to language and so he should not be taken as a philosopher of language.[8] This is obviously a misunderstanding of Frege because he did believe that language is fundamental to all human activities especially the activity of deductively inferring the logico-mathematical conclusions. It is quite true that Frege talks of thought as having a timeless logical domain and that the domain of thought is the domain of logic. But this does not prevent him from talking of a universal logical language that can truly represent the domain of thought. The fact that language transparently represents thought even in the form of a pure notation does underline the fact that thought is not independent of language, nor that we can grasp thought without language. Dummett[9] is right in telling that Frege is basically a philosopher of language since he raises the question of meaning only in the context of language. That is, he has taken sense as lying only in the representations of thought in language. For Frege, thoughts do not have sense because they themselves are the sense. Language has sense insofar as it expresses thought and so a study of thought is necessarily a study of language and *vice versa*. The interdependence of language and thought is so intimate that it is difficult to conceive one without the other. We have no recognition of thought if it were not manifested or expressed in language, and so thought is cognitively dependent on language. Besides, language itself is the vehicle of thought[10] and so it is nothing without the expression of thought.

Frege's well-known result in philosophy of language is his anti-psychologism which follows necessarily from his theory of logic. Logic, according to him, is not based on psychological principles. The logical laws are not derived from the mental operations since they are independent of how the human mind operates. Therefore Frege takes strong exception to those logicians who have converted all logical laws to the laws of psychology.[11] Psychologism reduces logic to psychology and to a subjective science. Frege writes :

But the expression "law of thought" seduces us into supposing that these laws are governing thinking in the same way as the laws of nature govern events in the external world. In that case they can be nothing but the laws of psychology, for thinking is a mental process. And if logic were concerned with those psychological laws it would be part of psychology; for it is in fact viewed in the same way.[12]

Against psychologism Frege has shown that the laws of thought which are the laws of logic are objective, eternal and are the necessary ground of all logical thinking. The logical laws constitute the foundations of mathematics.[13] Thus nothing is excluded from the domain of logic and the logical laws. Frege's logicism, though unsuccessful, is a landmark development in the history of philosophy of mathematics. It has not only demonstrated that logic is a universal domain of thought but also has shown that there is a universal language that represents the logical domain of thought.

Frege has taken the notion of representation as fundamental to his theory of language and thought. Language is itself the representation of thought in that thought remains obscure without the linguistic mirroring. In fact thought remains subjective in the absence of linguistic representation of it. That is, it remains subjective and private unless it is expressed in language. Thus thought and language go together to constitute the domain of logic. The laws of logic are the laws of both thought and language. So the objectivity of thought and language remains logically secure against the subjectivity of the psychological laws.

Frege admits that language is the only medium of expressing thought. Thought or sense is grasped in the judgements in language. That is why the sentences or judgements are the only vehicles of sense. Sentences themselves are the linguistic representations which are either true or false. In that sense they are representations of the world. Thus thought and language both are taken as the representations of the world. Frege has thereby shown that, since thought is the thought of the world, language as the vehicle of thought must itself be related to the world.

The notion of truth plays a significant role in the Fregean system of logic. It is because truth is the semantic concept that characterizes the linguistic representations. The latter either tell what the world is or fail to do so. In either case the notion of truth or its negation applies. This shows that logic is, generally speaking, the domain of truth,[14] that is, is the domain of linguistic representations that are either true or false. Besides, it is the domain of sense that explains how the linguistic representations are themselves possible. It is the notion of sense that holds the key to Frege's theory of language and logic.

Sense and Reference

Frege hit upon the sense-reference distinction in his investigation into the nature of thought, judgement and truth. His On Sense and Reference[15] was a turning point in his philosophical development, since it brought into focus the semantic duality between sense and reference so far as the structure of a judgement is concerned. A judgement and its constituents have both sense and reference. A judgement has a sense, that is, it expresses a thought insofar as it expresses something about the world. The sentence-constituents themselves also have sense in that they constitute the sense of the judgement expressed. Besides, a judgement has a reference in its truth-value. That is, the True and the False are the two truth-values which act as the referents[16] of the judgements. The sentence-constituents have the objects as their referents. Thus Frege arrives at a logical distinction between what is expressed and what is referred to in language. In his letter to Husserl dated 24 May 1891 Frege gives the following schema[17] of his important semantic discovery:

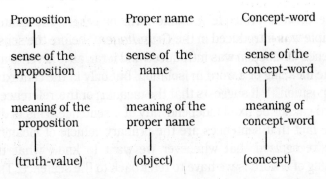

Proposition	Proper name	Concept-word
sense of the proposition	sense of the name	sense of the concept-word
meaning of the proposition	meaning of the proper name	meaning of concept-word
(truth-value)	(object)	(concept)

In this schema meaning and reference are taken as the same. Sense (*sinn*) and reference (*bedeutung*) are different not only in their content but also in their form. Sense is what is the judgemental content of the sentences whereas the reference is what is stood for by the those expressions.

The following theses follow as the corollary of Frege's distinction between sense and reference. They are,

A. Sentences are the primary vehicles of sense. Only derivatively the words have sense in the context of a sentence.

B. Sentences are also a species of names since, like names, they have reference.

C. Thought or sense is a logical entity existing independently of the world. It is the judgement that brings sense into contact with the world.

The thesis A is the famous context principle which is the cornerstone of Frege's semantics. It asserts the primacy of the sentences in language. The thesis B is the semantic monism that dissolves the duality between sentences and names. The thesis C is about the role of judgements and their truth-values in semantics.

Frege's semantics revolves round the thesis A as it adheres

to the context principle in some form or other. The context principle was introduced in the *Grundlagen*[18] before the sense-reference distinction was introduced and it ran as : "never to ask for the meaning of a word in isolation, but only in the context of a proposition".[19] It suggests that the meaning or the reference of a word cannot be fixed independently of a sentence. This is due to the fact that sentences are the primary vehicle of meaning. Frege recognized that whenever we want to know what the meaning of a word is we have to refer back to the sentence. This obviously leads to the fact that sentence-meaning is a composite thing such that only when we have word-meaning we can have the sentence-meaning built out of the former. This is what Dummett[20] calls the semantic molecularism in Frege's semantics.

The thesis B really marks a radical departure from conventional semantics in that it proposes semantic monism so far as name-sentence distinction is concerned. It results immediately in the idea that sentences and names both have reference. This, apparently, conflicts with the context principle which recognizes a distinction between words and sentences. The Fregean way out of this difficulty is that words are still different from sentences even if both share the function of referring. They refer in entirely different ways.

The thesis C really marks the emergence of the concept of truth in semantics. It suggests that truth is the mediating link between sense and the world. A judgement is the articulation of thought in relation to the world. That is, the judgement maps the sense onto the world in the form of an assertion or its denial. An assertion puts into language the apprehension of the ideal contents of thought in the context of the world. Here is what Frege calls the transition from the world of sense to the world of the empirical objects wherein truth appears as the mediating link. Semantics thus passes into the arena of the sentences and their truth-possibilities. The notion of representation becomes the central concept in the semantic theory.

Truth and Representations

Frege's semantics revolves round the concept of truth as it has been noted earlier. It reformulates the intuitive notion of truth without being bogged down in the metaphysical theories associated with it. Frege rejects the so-called correspondence theory of truth as he feels that any attempt to define truth leads to circularity. For him, truth remains indefinable.[21] Thus semantics must begin with a primitive category of truth, according to him.

The concept of truth, as it is understood semantically, has a core meaning in being the value of a representation. Truth itself is not a representation but it is the property of a representation so far as the latter is concerning the world. It may, however, be doubted whether, for Frege, truth is just a property of the assertions about the world. The idea of property is misleading in that it suggests, though wrongly, that it is a material property. But, for Frege, truth is a formal property. It is the semantic mark of an assertion being the correct representation of the world. Logic provides the laws of truth, and other formal features follow accordingly. This is evidently a formal question whether truth can be a substantial concept in semantics. In fact Frege leads us to believe that without truth there is no semantic distinction between a valid argument and an invalid one. The concept of logical truth pervades the whole domain of logic and language.

There is a strong tendency in Frege to elevate truth to the level of logical entities. This is because he admits that truth is the referent of the assertions. The referent is logically an object. So truth also is an object along with concepts and numbers all subsisting in the logical world. The Platonic world or the Fregean "third world"[22] houses all these abstract entities in their purity. But this need not refute the view that truth is a property since formal properties are equally objects in the logical sense and are also in the logical world. This argument does not deny the fact that, for Frege, truth logically matters and that the whole of logic is the domain of truth.

Frege makes a distinction between the world of thought and the world of empirical experience. The latter, which is otherwise known as the world of facts, is subsumed under the world of thought. That is why there is no independent category of fact in his system.[23] This may mean that truth is denied as one corresponding to the fact. But this is not the case. Truth is not taken as a correspondence at all. Truth is the formal property of all indicative sentences. So true sentences are so-called by virtue of their relation to the world. Logical truths themselves are true by virtue of their meaning alone. Frege thus makes it clear that truth is indicative of the world or the reality.

However, the notion of truth is logically linked with the linguistic representations of the reality. This is because we cannot judge anything true or false without introducing the concept of judgement or assertion. This is supposed to be due to the fact that thought is apprehended in the judgement and then made manifest in the linguistic assertions. The world makes appropriate inroad into the assertions themselves thus making them either true or false. Frege writes,

> An advance in science usually takes place in this way, first a thought is apprehended, such as can perhaps be expressed in a sentence-question, and, after appropriate investigations, this thought is finally recognized to be true. We declare the recognition of truth in the form of an indicative sentence.[24]

The progression from thought to truth is the story of truth unfolding itself. Truth, though immanent in thought, is fully manifest only in the assertion of an indicative sentence. Thus truth is fully involved in the linguistic representation of the world. Truth becomes what it is only when it is world-looking. This is what Frege puts in other words when he says that truth does not add anything to the sentence except that it tells what the world actually is. He says,

So it seems, then, that nothing is added to the thought by my ascribing to it the property of truth, and yet is it not a great result when the scientist after much hesitation and careful inquiry can finally say "what I suppose is true"? The meaning of the word 'true' seems to be altogether unique.[25]

The uniqueness of truth lies in the fact that it is always other-looking. It is not the thought-content itself. It is what makes the thought-content representational. It can be seen that truth is not created by the cognizer because it is not a product of the acts of cognition. It is objective in that it tells what the world is though it itself does not belong to the world.[26]

The notion of truth is thus related to the world in such a way that whenever we make an assertion true or false we are relating it to the world. The world is very much in the language-game of assertion because, without the latter, the question of assertion does not arise. As Frege has made it clear, truth does not add anything to the assertion itself though it tells how the world is when the sentence is true. This is also what follows logically when we take assertions as affirmative or negative. The question of truth is embedded in the logic of assertions.

We are, in fact, searching for the notion of representation in the Fregean theory of truth and sense. The notion of representation is evident in the idea that truth and assertions go together. Without the assertions being the representations of the world, we cannot talk about truth at all. A true assertion is a true representation as well. This makes further evident the concept of representation in the notion of sense itself. Sense, as we have already seen, is thought and thought itself is the thought about the world. Thus thought and reality are logically related in that the former is the representation of the latter. The representational relation is not that of copying or putting the reality as it is. It is rather telling what the world logically is. This notion of logical representationality is the core of Frege's concept of sense.

Frege's main concern is to relate thought to the world. Though he assumes that thought is eternal, yet it is supposed to be related to the world. Thoughts are in a sense incomplete until they are brought to the world through the linguistic assertions. Language makes thoughts this-worldly in that they relate to the assertion-conditions in which the judgements are made. In this way logic, which is the domain of thoughts, is made the basis of how the assertions are made about the world.

Language thus becomes the focal point of Frege's logic and semantics since in language alone the notion of representation takes its roots. It explains why logic becomes more interested in how sense is expressed in language. It is, in fact, a scandal to say that Fregean thoughts are pre-linguistic and must be filtered through a linguistic mechanism.[27] In fact these thoughts are linguistic in being expressed in language and are to be asserted or denied in the world. The so-called "Third World" in Fregean logic is at best a metaphor. That shows the emptiness of the claim that Frege never bothered about the world as his interest was in the thoughts in themselves rather than in how thoughts are true or false.

In fact, if our claims about the nature of truth and representation are valid, then the central point of Frege's theory of language is the representation itself. This is evident in the idea of there being true or false assertions about the world. The assertions are so framed that they posit the different ways in which we can relate our thoughts to the world. The sense of the assertions is that exact way in which the world is projected into language. Frege's concern was to locate truth in the linguistic projections that language makes concerning the world. Therefore the semantics of assertions is the semantics of how best truth can be secured for the assertions in the background of their relation with the world.

Sense, Logic and the World

Truth being the single most concept for the Fregean semantics that brings the assertions and their sense face-to-face with the world, now the question arises, can the sense itself which is supposed to be an ontological entity be related to the world? Frege believes that sense is an ontological entity that is self-existent and autonomous in that it does not depend on the world for its existence. Sense is ontologically secure against the contingent world which is itself dependent on the categories of the mind for its significance. Though Frege does not say so, he definitely means that the world is in need of the logical categories which systematize its structure. The world does not have more entities than logic can anticipate. This is reflected in Frege's Kantian dictum that sense or thought determines reference. Besides, the very fact that the objects and the concepts make up the world shows that the categories make a difference to the world. In this respect, it is noteworthy that sense is like the categories *a priori* and so, epistemically as well as ontologically, prior to the world.

However, the ontological status of sense suggests a deep gulf between what is the thought or significance of the sentences and their actual application in the world. Sense in that sense remains basically self-contained. But this may mean that sense is the pre-linguistic entity that needs language to be related to the world. Language itself being a contingent phenomenon may sometimes fail to express sense. This way of looking at Frege does conflict with the idea that, for him, language is basic and that sense is embedded in language. Dummett therefore supposes that the Fregean sense is primarily epistemological since Frege is concerned with the cognitive grasp of sense in language and thus of its application in the world.[28] This of course does not mean that sense, for Dummett, is a mental entity or, for that matter, something in the consciousness. The anti-psychologist argument remains valid in Frege for all practical purposes. Hence it can be said that sense is a non-mental and a non-physical entity and in short an entity of the logical sort.

The ontology of sense that residually remains in Frege does not make any difference to the logico-semantic doctrine that sense is expressed in language and is related to the world. This makes the task of logic easier in finding out the link between language and the world. As we have seen earlier, the domain of logic is the domain of necessary truths regarding the relation of ideas and their sentential expressions. In that case they are the complete expressions of sense in its logical structure. But that itself entails that sense makes demands on the world so far as the sentences are regarding the world. Sense, in fact, systematizes the world and orders it into a coherent world. Thus logic is the underlying domain of the logical laws.

Logic is, for Frege, the domain of necessity in that it only takes into account the logical structure of language and the world. Language and the world are basically well-ordered but, because of the exigency of their articulation, they are apparently not so. This therefore invites the logician to tell that the sense underlying language must reflect that order which is ontologically there. This discovery of sense in language is the only way we can go about finding the structure of the world. That demonstrates that logic is the method of discovering sense and thereby discovering the logical form of the world.

Now the question arises, if sense and logic go together, how is it that sense remains pre-linguistic as believed by some? Admittedly, sense is linguistic in that it is expressed in language and there is its necessary connection with the world. In that case it is illogical to say that sense is in a metaphysical world. Frege discourages the tendency to make sense inaccessible to language and logic. This is evidenced in his semantic treatment of sense and his theory of logical grammar that provides a defence of his theory of sense.[29]

The theory of logical grammar outlines the broad contours of the theory of sense; the former is meant to show that language matters to logic and sense. Without language there is nothing called logic as such since logic itself provides a language that goes beyond the confines of the ordinary language of the common speaker. That shows that the thoughts or the senses, which are the logical entities, must themselves be articulated in language in a transparent medium. Logical language is the transparent medium for thought. We have so far indicated that the transparent medium is the universal medium of sense.

The question of representation becomes inevitable in view of the fact that truth follows from sense. Truth is necessarily related to the representations in that the latter have to be either true or false assertion about the world. Sense is the ground of all language-use and in that sense, it is the ground of truth as well. That is, sense is that which defines the truth-conditions of the assertions. Truth-conditions are the immediately available indicators of sense and thus a link can be established between sense and truth-conditions.[30]

Wittgenstein and Transcendental Logic

The Fregean theory of logic and grammar is the background of Wittgenstein's *Tractatus* that develops a representational framework for understanding language and the world. The structure of sense is the main concern, since it provides the key to the structure of language and the world. According to Wittgenstein, the structure of the world is the same as the structure of language and this can be unfolded by the logical structure of sense. This is the source of the idea that logic is transcendental since it brings out the underlying structures of language and the world.[31] What Frege intended, but never executed, is attempted by Wittgenstein in his transcendental conception of logic which aims at bringing out the essence of language and the world.

The notions of sense and representation constitute the starting point of Wittgenstein's logic. For him, logic studies the necessary structures of language and its sense. That is, logic investigates the inner necessities governing language. This results in what may be called the logical grammar of language and their necessary rules. The *Tractatus* represents the idea of logical grammar in its complete form in that it abolishes the duality between the grammar of ordinary language and that of the ideal language. For it, language is the one given, once for all, in nature and so the grammar that we talk about is the only one we can have. Thus there arises the need of a grammar of the necessary rules of language.

All the rules of language are, however, the rules of linguistic representations in that language is a representation of the world. Wittgenstein realizes that the idea of representation is inevitable for grammar since there is no other way we can conceive language at all. Language is the way we relate ourselves to the world and it is the way the world is mirrored in a network of symbols. This fact is a necessary fact about language in that language is a method of expressing what is given in the world. The world is existing independently of language but, so far as the structure of the world is concerned, there is the inevitability of bringing it out in the structure of the language through a study of the logical grammar of language. Hence the necessity of the representational structure of language.

The notion of representation is particularly significant as the notion of sense or meaning is embedded in it. The logical relation between the two is this: sense as the logicl thought expressed in a proposition is the thought of the world, that is, of the facts that constitute the world. The world itself is open-ended but, as soon as the world is made intelligible, we have to recognize that there is nothing in it which is not anticipated by logic. In fact, logic is said to be the mirror-image of the world.[32] The latter concept suggests that the world has a determinate structure that can be logically mapped. This underlying assumption leads Wittgenstein to take language as a representation or mirror of the world. The world, for that matter, does not cease to be a contingent world but, so far as logic is concerned, the necessary structure of the world is all that matters. As Wittgenstein tells, the domain of logic is the domain of necessity and of logical laws which give us the picture of the world that obeys the laws of logic.[33]

Two ideas dominate the new conception of logic, namely, the idea of representationality and the idea of universality. The first idea is that of the sense-world connection, i.e., the connection of the propositions with the facts through the representationality of the former. This makes sense the inner content of the propositions such that, once the sentence expressing the sense is made, the sense is fully grasped. This leads Wittgenstein to say that sense is very much a part of the inner logic of the proposition. This inner logic is the logic of representationality of sense.

The second idea is of the universality of the logical structure of sense. The logical form of sense is the logical form of every expression whatsoever. That is to say, every linguistic expression reflects a sense as it is representationally connected with the world. From this it can be inferred that sense is the universal logical form of language and as such is the bedrock of the linguistic representation of the world. The latter idea is the underlying theme of the theory of sense. Wittgenstein believes that without the universality thesis there is no way we can prove that language is representational at all.

However, the greatest hurdle to such a theory is that language, as it is contingently given, may not be universalizable, that is, that it cannot be shown to be representational in every aspect. The Fregean assertions could be shown to be representational but not the discourse that treats of emotions or the feelings. Wittgenstein therefore took to the idea that it is the propositions that represent facts irrespective of their content and subject-matter. The facts are formal in their structure and so they are the subject-matter of the linguistic representations. The universality of the representational framework is built into language in the logical sense. Language as such is representational in its relation to the world.

The Picture Theory

The central concern of Wittgenstein's transcendental logic is the picture theory that brings out the logical structure of the world in and through the structure of language. The latter, i.e., the structure of language is the key to the former, i.e., the structure of the world. This is a transcendental thesis in that through logic alone is the structure of the world mapped. That is, in the logical structure of language is represented the structure of the world. Wittgenstein makes it clear that the essence of the world could not be mapped in the thought-structure unless the latter is the one reflected in language. Thus there is the inevitability about the idea that language is the ultimate ground of the possibility of our knowledge of the world.

The picture theory is the grammatical articulation of the fact that language makes the world intelligible to us. That is, it lays down under what conditions the world is transparent to us. These conditions are those which Frege called the conditions of sense as applicable to the linguistic representations. These conditions lay in the fact that sense is propositional and is regarding the world. However, Frege did not make these conditions sufficiently logical and intrinsic to language and there remained a gap between what the propositions say and what the world is. The picture theory remedies this situation by making sense transparent, that is, by making the sense of a proposition agree with the world on all fours. This can happen only when the logical form of the proposition agrees with the logical form of the world. The picture theory tells in so many words that the underlying logical structure of language and the world is the same. Though this is a highly metaphysical thesis, it is the basis of the semantics and the syntax of the picture theory. The theory itself is both a syntactic and a semantic thesis in that it lays down the logical conditions of the linguistic symbols and their interrelations. Besides, it tells what the symbols mean and stand for. Both these conditions coincide because the syntactic devices themselves are the articulations of the sense of the symbols.

In the *Tractatus* the semantic conditions of sense are more open than in Frege. Frege made them the conditions of the truth of the propositions. So here the concept of truth and truth-conditions is paramount such that if the proposition is understood its truth-conditions are also equally understood. But in Wittgenstein these semantic conditions are on the surface since the grammatical structures of the propositions are so articulate that they take care of the sense and truth-conditions as well. Thereby the semantic conditions are not rejected but are made logically secure so far as their relation to the world is concerned. The difference with Frege's semantics lies in this that, whereas, in Frege, the truth-conditions and sense hang in the balance, in Wittgenstein they are made rooted in the world through a picture theory. There is both a syntactic and semantic guarantee that sense is related to the world through the propositions which are the representations of the world.

The following are the main theses of the picture theory as a theory of logical grammar and as a theory of sense:

A. Every well-formed proposition is a logical representation of the world. It is a syntactic articulation of the world as it is logically conceived.

B. The world is the totality of what is real and logically conceivable. Thus language which represents the world is meaningful if and only if it has all the syntactic and semantic resources required. That includes a theory of logical grammar and also a theory of sense.

The thesis A is the general picture theory that tells that there is a universality about the idea that language is a picture of the world in the logical sense. This aspect of the theory is best depicted in its assumption that language and the world have the same logical form. The thesis B, on the other hand, is a special theory of grammar that tells under what conditions the propositions are pictures. There is underlying this thesis the idea of depiction which is one of the semantic conditions of the proposition being a picture of the world.

The logic of depiction introduces the concept of projection as the central concept of the theory of representation. Here there is the requirement that the depicted reality is of the same logical genre as the depicting medium. That is to say, if the proposition is the depicting medium, the fact which is depicted must be propositional and linguistically articulateable. That is the essence of the proposition and the fact. Wittgenstein says,

> The general propositional form is the essence of the proposition.
>
> To give the essence of a proposition means to give the essence of all description, and thus the essence of the world.[34]

This is the logical theory that the essence of the world and the essence of language are the same. This marks the emergence of the idea that language is the model of the world and that it presents the logical scaffolding of the latter.

The idea of model goes back to the scientific and mathematical notion of the model[35] which is the bedrock of the modern concept of science that tries to understand the world through various mathematical devices. Wittgenstein's picture theory provides a grammatical theory of model to suggest that all the scientific and mathematical models are ultimately linguistic. For example, the Newtonian mechanical model "is an attempt to construct according to a single plan all the true propositions that we need for the depiction of the world".[36] Thus model-making ultimately goes into the heart of all linguistic depiction of the reality. This is the special grammatical theory that the picture theory leads to.

The general form of the picture theory remains grammatical and yet it tells that the only relation between language and the world is that of representation of the latter by the former. The crucial notion is the notion of representation that goes into the centre of the theory of language. Now the question arises, why is it that language at all be so related to the world? Could it not be the case that world is otherwise represented than though language? Wittgenstein's answer is that there is no question of asking whether language could be dispensed with as a medium of representation because that presupposes as it were we could go beyond language to answer this question. But that is impossible because what is beyond language is nonsensical. So there is no sense in supposing that language might not have been the representation of the world.

Language is endowed with rich semantic and syntactic resources to represent the world. This is what the picture theory eminently emphasizes. This follows from the fact that there is a projectional possibility for every aspect of reality. The facts in the world are all-comprehensive to include everything in reality, and language has the corresponding names for all these constituents of reality. Thus a logical harmony between the world and language is present throughout the language-world correlations. This logical harmony is another name for the metaphysical harmony between language and the world.[37] The picture theory is the theory of this harmony primarily and it tells that the logic of world-representation lies in the logic of language. This is the transcendental thesis underlying the picture theory.

Sense and the World-Order

The picture theory makes it redundant that there is a theory of sense independently of the theory of propositions. The sense is the sense of propositions and there is no other way of locating it except through the understanding of the propositions. The sense is the thought contained in the proposition and therefore it is not an extra-propositional entity at all. Besides, sense is not a factual entity in that it is not found along with other facts in the world. Thus Wittgenstein grants autonomy to sense in the sense that sense or significance of the propositions is self-guaranteed rather than dependent on the world.

Sense in that sense is a linguistic reality or, if we can say so, it is a logical entity. Its logicality follows from its propositional origin. This is evidenced in the idea that sense is shown or expressed in the structure of the proposition.[38] That is, sense is the essential logical form of a proposition which makes the latter a picture of the fact it states. Wittgenstein provides a logical deduction of the sense by proving that without it the proposition cannot be articulated at all. Propositions are so-called because of their inherent formal character to represent the world-phenomena. That is the reason we can as well find a metaphysical ground of why sense must be independently real. Any way, it is the logical status of sense that is so important for the semanticist and the logician.

For Wittgenstein, as for Frege, the domain of sense is the domain of logic since the latter alone can study the formal character of the representations to which the sense pertains. It is evident that sense is the formal essence of the propositions and this cannot be studied except by logic which aims at showing what the essence of language and the world is. Logic as such is autonomous in that it "takes care of itself"[39] as it unfolds the inner logic of language and the world. This is Wittgenstein's continuation of the Fregean idea that in logic nothing is relevant except the necessary laws governing language and thought.

Wittgenstein is preoccupied with the idea that logic is also unfolding the structure of the world by unfolding the structure of language. This makes him see that sense of the propositions is intrinsically related to the world. Sense as the thought-content is concerning the world insofar as the thought is the thought of the world. But this relation is nothing mental as it is through linguistic representations that sense gets into the world. The linguistic representations are so structured that they carry the essence of the world and in that alone the sense of the propositions enters the network of the world. Thus sense becomes part of the world-essence and through that the world gets meaningfully represented in language. The world is such that it is thinkable and representable in language and in this the notion of sense plays a crucial role.

The realism associated with the theory of sense lays down that nothing is wrong with the autonomy of sense as long as we do not separate sense from language. Besides, if sense is real in language it cannot but be true of the world. This is because language is itself intrinsically related with the world. Hence the gap between sense and the world-order is further bridged so as to make sense the essence of the world-representation. This can be characterized as the semantic harmony between what is posited as the sense and what is given as the fact in the world. The fact is a construction in language in terms of the logical form of language. So facts themselves show the marks of the logical shadow of sense on the world. In this sense the world is the world of sense and inner necessity. That does not, however, abolish the contingency of the world. But logic makes a difference to this world by making it linguistically representable.

Wittgenstein's theory of sense underwent little change in his later works. The problem continues to be one of making sense relevant to the world. Though the propositions are the locus of sense there is an inner boundary built around sense in the structure of the language-game such that sense becomes the unfoldment of the grammar of the language-game. Sense is the grammatical essence of language such that the world-order is posited in the grammatical network itself. This is the inner dynamics of sense that outlines the logic of the world though the contents of the thoughts embodied in language. There is thus a continuity between the *Tractatus* and Wittgenstein's later philosophy so far as the notion of sense is concerned.

Semantic Holism

The later theory of language and sense in Wittgenstein is holistic in that it integrates language-use and sense in a more comprehensive system. The Tractarian domain of propositions which instantiated the logical contents of sense is now transformed into the domain of the language-games which equally makes sense available in the structure of language. While the propositions in the logical language remained on the same level there appeared to be a hierarchy on the surface in the *Tractatus*. This is now abolished by Wittgenstein in his theory of an integral system of language-games. The language-games constitute a system even if they do not share anything more than a family resemblance. The concept of family resemblance contains the idea of unity which is the bedrock of all language-games. Since the language-games do not fall apart and hold together, they are logically united in a system.

Wittgenstein's holism[40] is the doctrine that language cannot be bifurcated into unrelated items, though, as units of language, they are relatively independent. It is the relative independence that has led people to believe that there is complete disunity in the system of language itself. The semantic molecularists have taken the clue from Frege and have claimed that language is a hierarchical order[41] such that there can be no single theory of meaning for all orders of language. This can be a misrepresentation of Wittgenstein's theory of language since he has claimed that language is like an organic structure that has a natural history[42] of its own. If language is an organic structure, it cannot have components which are dissociated from one another. The logic of holism is that which imposes a unified structure on language though not in the way Quine[43] has visualized. Quine has claimed holism for the conceptual scheme rather than for language and so in that sense he and Wittgenstein do not meet.

Semantic holism introduces a theory of sense according to which there is no isolated phenomenon called sense or meaning. Meaning belongs to the whole of a language-game and is itself a whole in the sense that it is neither a composite entity nor is it a single content. As a single content, it could be an entity either in the mind or in the world. But both the possibilities are ruled out. Meaning is not a composite whole either. This is the case because meaning is not constructed by a method of assimilation. As Wittgenstein has argued, meaning is the physiognomy of the language[44] such that there is a definite way of locating it in the language-use itself. Language-use is the locus of meaning but not a product of use. Thus sense is not a single-event phenomenon but a multidimensional phenomenon. That accounts for its holistic character.

Semantic holism thus provides a better framework for understanding meaning in view of the fact that it takes meaning away from the facts of the world and puts it back in the language itself. That is, it makes meaning accountable to language and language alone instead of making it world-dependent. Meaning in this sense is the linguistic phenomenon that needs no accounting for except a kind of fixing in the overall network of language. Sense, in the total context of language, appears to be something spread over the language rather than is an entity in the world or in the mind. This is the idea that meaning is not to be searched for as something to be discovered and so as something hidden[45] in the secret of the human understanding. The idea of hidden something arises when it is forgotten that meaning is lying on the surface and is made manifest in the language-use itself. Wittgenstein is struggling to ensure that meaning is open to the language-user in the public space of grammar itself.

Now the question arises, is meaning better secured against scepticism and relativism in the holistic framework? If meaning is on the surface, can it not be the case that it is something absolutely ephemeral and also something dependent on the perceiver? This possibility is ruled out by Wittgenstein in his private language argument where he argues that meaning is not something which is dependent on the cognizer and his or her preferences. Besides, it is not something which we decide to have. So subjectivism is not a real threat to meaning-holism. What threatens meaning-holism is the possibility of meaning-indeterminacy which Quine has envisaged. But this possibility also can be ruled out in view of the fact that meaning is not man-dependent since it is a linguistic phenomenon and is governed by grammatical necessity. Meaning, for that matter, is the stable and grammatically necessary phenomenon such that the more it is realized in the stream of life and language, the deeper it appears to be embedded in the linguistic rules. This is the logical compulsion of holism that meaning becomes a part of a larger scenario and that it is the overriding desideratum of language as a whole.

Wittgenstein's semantic framework, in continuation with the Fregean framework, makes room for the reality of sense in a linguistic sense. But he adds that the sense must be deeply laid in our language and life. That is to say that sense must be laid within the language-games which are the given schemes of language-use. Sense, in this way, is shown in the language-games. Meaning in a way speaks for itself in that we cognize it as soon as we see it. No further explanation is necessary.[46]

Logic of Representations

The ultimate goal of the meaning theory is a theory of representations. Therefore it is necessary to evaluate the possibility of the theory of representations in view of semantic holism we have examined earlier. Two things emerge on the scene, namely, the nature of language-game as a method of representation and the availability of sense in the language-games. As said earlier, language-games are the holistic linguistic phenomena that carry the methods of representation. In them alone the sense appears in its full glory.

To call language-games the methods of representations is to say that in language alone there is the talk of representation. Representation is the grammatical activity of talking of something in the world. It is a way of saying something rather than nothing. That is the way of putting a thought-content in the linguistic framework. Of course it is not that thought is independent of language but that language alone represents what thought itself is. Thus to say something is to think and speak, that is, to use language. This act of language-use is the act of representing something in the world.

The world is the other pole of language-use since the language-user is not enough. The user of language is the one who makes the grammatical moves and thus is the rule-follower. But his rule-following is given in the background of language-learning in the world. Thus the world is the ever present reality which suggests the necessity of rule-following. If the world would not be there, there would be no necessity of following any rule since everything becomes arbitrary. Logic and grammar would make no sense in case there is no world[47] since what shall we talk about in the absence of the world? So the world is the necessary partner in the language-use and rule-following.

But how shall the world be represented? Is it that it is represented so that we only describe it in so many words? This is what Frege felt when he said that truth is the goal of logic. For him, only truth matters in language. Thus, in Frege, we have the predominance of assertions. But Wittgenstein felt that this is not always the case. Though the propositions are pictures of reality, they need not be pictures of the same kind. Hence, in the *Tractatus*, it is held that propositions are logical pictures of reality in very different ways. But this appeared to be too Fregean to be against the predominance of truth and assertions. So a more radical turn was made to show that language-games alone can be taken as the ways of world-representation. The demand is no more that we describe the world in our language. Rather, it is now necessary to throw open the world to language as it is, that is, to make it available in the natural language-formations. The latter are the language-games which dot our language as so many formations in which the representation of the world takes place.

Now language and the world stand together in a unique bond of mutual partnership. The problem is no more of making the world conspicuous in grammar but of seeing the world in the conspicuous grammar itself.[48] The latter is the sum-total of the grammatical relations and their necessary rules in which the world is already present in its logical form. This is the underlying principle of representation which we have taken for granted. Semantics which cannot but be holistic is based on this principle that language is the only way we can make the world available to us.

References

1. **See** Van Heijenoort,"Logic as Calculus and Logic as Language", in *Synthese* 17 (1967), pp. 324-30.

2. Frege, *The Basic Laws of Arithmetic*, tr. and ed. by M. Furth (University of California Press, Berkeley and Los Angeles, 1964), p. 12.

3. *Ibid.*

4. Frege, *Conceptual Notation*, tr. by T.W. Bynum (Clarendon Press, Oxford,1972).

5. **See** the Preface to the *Conceptual Notation*, pp.105-06.

6. *Ibid.*

7.   *See* Baker and Hacker, *Frege: Logical Excavations* (Blackwell, Oxford, !9840) for such a view which puts Frege's philosophy in the pre-linguistic stage of philosophy.

8.   *Ibid.*

9.   *See* Dummett, *The Interpretation of Frege's Philosophy* (Duckworth, London, 1981) for a defence of the view that Frege is basically a philosopher of language.

10. *Ibid. See* Wittgenstein, *Philosophical Investigations*, tr. by G.E. M. Anscombe (Blackwell, Oxford, 1953).

11. *See* Frege, *The Basic Laws of Arithmetic* especially the Introduction, pp. 1-25. *Also see* Frege, *The Foundations of Arithmetic*, tr. by J.L. Austin (Blackwell, Oxford, 1950).

12. Frege, *The Basic Laws of Arithmetic*, pp. 12-13.

13. *Ibid.*

14. Cf. *Posthumous Writings*, ed. by H. Hermes, F. Kambartel and F. Kaulbach (Blackwell, Oxford, 1979).

15. Frege, "On Sense and Reference" in *Translations from the Philosophical Writings of Gottlob Frege* tr. by P. T. Geach and M. Black (Blackwell, Oxford, 1952).

16. *Ibid.*

17. Frege, *Philosophical and Mathematical Correspondence*, ed. by Gabriel, Hermes, Kambartel, Theil and Veraart, tr. by Hans Kaal (Blackwell, Oxford, 1980), p. 63.

18. *See* Frege, *The Foundations of Arithmetic*, Introduction.

19. *Ibid.*, p. x.

20. *See* Dummett, *Frege, Philosophy of Language* (Duckworth, London, 1973).

21. Frege, "The Thought: An Enquiry", in *Philosophical Logic*, ed. by P. F. Strawson (Oxford University Press, Oxford, 1967).

22. *Ibid.*

23. *Ibid.*

24. *Ibid.*, p. 22.

25. *Ibid.*, pp. 20-21.

26. *Ibid.*

27. **See** Paul Schweizer, "Blind Grasping and Fregean Senses", in *Philosophical Studies* 62 (1991), pp. 263-87.

28. Cf. Durnmett, *Frege, Philosophy of Language.*

29. Cf. Frege, "Logic", in *Posthumous Writings*, pp.1-8.

30. Cf. Dummett, *Frege, Philosophy of Language.*

31. Wittgenstein, *Tractatus Logico-Philosophicus* tr. by D.F. Pears and B.F. McGuinness (Routledge and Kegan Paul, London,1961),6.13. (Henceforward to be abbreviated as *Tractatus*).

32. *Ibid.*

33. *Ibid.* 2.012, 6.3.

34. *Ibid.* 5.471-5.4711.

35. Cf. *Ibid.* 6.34-6.342.

36. *Ibid.* 6.343.

37. Cf. Wittgenstein, *Zettel,* tr. by G. E. M. Anscombe (Blackwell, Oxford, 1967) sect. 55 :

    Like everything metaphyasical the harmony between thought and reality is to be found in the grammar of the language.

38. *Tractatus* 4.°22.

39. *Ibid.* 5.473. **See also** Wittgenstein, *Notebooks* 1914-16, tr. by G.E.M. Anscombe (Blackwell, Oxford, 1961), p. 2.

40. **See** D.F. Pears, "Wittgenstein's Holism", in *Dialectica* 44 (1990), pp. 165-73.

41. Cf. Dummett, "What is a Theory of Meaning?", in *Mind and Language,* ed. by S. Guttenplan (Blackwell, Oxford, 1975), p. 97-138.

42. **See** Wittgenstein, *Philosophical Investigations* I sect.25 and II, xii.

43. W. V. Quine, " Two Dogmas of Empiricism", in *From a Logical Point of View* (Harvard Univerity Press, Cambridge, Massachusetts, 1953).

44.   Cf. Wittgenstein, *Philosophical Investigations* I, sect.568.

45.   *Ibid.* **See also** Norman Malcolm, *Wittgenstein: Nothing is Hidden* (Blackwell, Oxford,1986).

46.   Cf. *Philosophical Investigations* I, sect.654 :

     Our mistake is to look for an explanation where we ought to look at what happens as a "proto-phenomenon". That is, where we ought to have said : This language-game is played.

47.   Cf. *Tractatus*, 5.5521.

48.   Cf. *Philosophical Investigations*, sects.122 and 371-373.

3

The Structure of Representations II

THE theory of representations has got a new phase of life in the philosophy of language developed by Davidson and Dummett in recent times though in entirely different directions. Davidson represents the semantic tradition which can be traced back to Tarski and beyond, perhaps to Frege, though he is rooted in the naturalistic tradition owing allegiance to Quine. Davidson combines two traditions in his philosophy, namely, the one identified with the rationalist tradition in semantics with a firm commitment to the classical notion of truth and the other being the tradition of empiricism and naturalism which demands empirical verification for the semantic theory. Reconciling the two traditions is not easy but Davidson has achieved a balance between the two in his theory of representations. According to him, language is a rational mode of representing the world and evaluating the assertions about the world in the standardly available method of truth-schematization in logic. Logic is in the background supplying the laws of truth to assess the various ways the world is represented. Thus Davidson has made it mandatory that language is basically the system of representations which tells how the world is. Though it is the case that he does not accept the scheme-content distinction in the way the empiricists do, he does not deny that language and world are uniquely related and that truth-assessment of the assertions about the world is the subject-matter of the semantic theory.

Dummett provides an alternative theory of representations without being committed to the classical notion of truth and the idea that truth is the basic desideratum of semantics. He disowns the Davidsonian discourse of the semantically given and opts for the semantic reconstruction of the notion of meaning and the assertability of the linguistic representations. According to Dummett, the world is represented in language and is therefore under the semantic control of our assertions and their intersubjective conditions. Dummett characterizes his semantic standpoint as anti-realist as he proposes to dispense with the metaphysical realist's contention that truth and the world are independent of the cognizer. His theory thus goes against the theory that the classical notion of truth is sufficiently well grounded to supply the right method for assessing the linguistic representations. In his theory of representations there is the intuitionist leaning towards the creative synthesis of language and our conceptual structures so far as the semantic assessments of our linguistic representations are concerned. The notion of truth and meaning are so designed as to tell not what the factual content of a proposition is but how much we have contributed to the emergence of meaning and truth.

The aim of this chapter is not to give an exegesis of the semantics of Davidson and Dummett but to reconstruct the theory of representations to provide an answer to the primary question whether meaning is representational.

Truth and the Rationality of the Semantic Discourse

Davidson is a philosopher of truth and the rationality of the semantic discourse. He makes truth the foundation of meaning and so of the intelligibility of language. The latter being the primary task of the philosopher Davidson takes truth as the key to the understanding and interpretation of language. The logic of interpretation is the logic of truth according to him. There are two ways in which truth could be related to the discourse, namely, the transcendent and the immanent ways. Truth as a transcendent feature of language was emphasized by the classical semanticists and logicians. For them, truth transcends all that the language-user does and so is little affected by the conditions of linguistic assertions. Truth in that sense is cognition-transcendent and metaphysically sealed against any human contingency. Frege, following Plato, perhaps believed that truth is logical and independent of the cognitive grasp of the knower[1] and thus propounded the semantic theory that secures truth against all the epistemological odds.

Frege was, however, aware that truth is cognitively available to the language-user. This insight in Frege was emphasized by Wittgenstein in his early and later philosophy so as to prove that truth is immanent in the very structure of the propositions which are the representations of the world. Thus, truth as an immanent category, belongs to language and, as Wittgenstein would have put it, it belongs to the language-game of assertions.[2] Quine further gave a radical push to the concept of truth by making it the property of an immanent grammar.[3] In Quine's holistic framework, truth was made synonymous with the method of appraisal of the conceptual structures *vis-a-vis* our experience of the world. Truth, in Quine, becomes one of the semantic concepts that quietly operates as a method of rationalizing our discourse.

Davidson follows Quine in naturalizing semantics and truth making truth as the immanent feature of language. Davidson turns the conceptual holism of Quine into the holistic theory of language and truth.[4] He places truth right at the centre of the semantics of natural language and makes it the pivotal concept so far as the assessment of the linguistic representations is concerned. While, however, Frege, Wittgenstein and Quine take the concept of truth largely as disquotational, Davidson takes it as an axiomatizable phenomenon that can be captured in the Tarskian schema and can thus be made the internal feature of natural language. Davidson is more forward-looking, positive and system-building so far as truth is concerned unlike his predecessors.

The immanent theory of truth tells that truth resides in how a statement or assertion is made rather than in what makes the latter true. That is, truth is the business of the speaker rather than of the world. The world is neutral to whether we make true or false assertions, though it stands in the background of both. The statements as such could not be without truth-values and so it is an immanent feature of them that they are truth-characterizable. Davidson makes truth the central concept in his system such that it is the most indispensable concept so far as semantics of natural language is concerned.

However, Davidson approaches the concept of truth not in the intuitive way but through the metasemantic discourse of Tarski who defines truth through a system of logical categories. Tarski[5] attempted to define truth in an elaborate way to lay down the logical structure of semantics. His aim was precisely to find out how truth can be defined for the formal languages which are constructed for the purpose of making scientific semantics possible. So he took meaning and other logical categories for granted and made every effort to define truth through the accepted categories. But Davidson has made no effort to define truth either for the formalized languages or for the natural languages. He takes for granted that truth is a primitive concept[6] and that it is immanent to natural language. Nevertheless he finds the Tarskian metasemantics worth taking seriously for the reason that truth is important even for Tarski. Davidson begins with truth and goes forward to provide a method of interpretation for language in general in order to introduce the concept of meaning. According to him, the concept of meaning is problematic because there is no definite method of understanding it. So his effort is to provide the method to understand meaning and this he finds in the theory of truth.

For Davidson truth belongs to the semantic structure of language and therefore is the most primitive category that semantics can think of. That is why there is no question of defining truth for the language at all. Davidson starts off with the notion of truth because that is how he can define meaning and intelligibility of language. But that is possible only if there is a logical structure of language already available and that can be stated in a metalanguage. Truth, is after all, a metalinguistic term, that is, it is only in a logical framework that it can be displayed. This is a Tarskian legacy which Davidson accepts but it does not commit him to the theory that the metalanguage is a higher order language. Metalanguage is, for him, a part of the natural language that has a logical structure as its innermost logical form. Davidson thus accepts the fact that there is only one language that contains both the object-language and meta-language. In short, language is as such universal in having within it its own metalanguage.[7] This theory of language suggests that truth is bound to be immanent to language since we can never go beyond language to define truth. For Tarski, truth is external to language as it can be defined only in a higher order language. This leads to the possibility that language could per chance have been without truth as a category, or, at best, that truth is accidental to the language-system. This Davidson denies by the theory that truth is internal and immanent to language.

Davidson declares truth to be a substantive category rather than a mere accidental property of statements. This is to say that truth belongs to the formal or logical structure of sentences that are the statements about the world. Truth does not accrue to the sentences accidentally but necessarily in that, without being either true or false, the sentences themselves do not exist. This

Davidson proves by showing that the truth-predicate applies to sentences only when there is adequate knowledge of the fact that there is a satisfaction of the same in the world. The notion of satisfaction is Tarski's but Davidson has employed it in order to avoid using the concept of fact. Facts are far too metaphysical to do the job. So the concept of satisfaction does the indispensable job of relating the sentences to the world.[8] As Davidson realizes, truth is not merely a relation between language and the world but something more than that in that truth indicates how inextricably the assertions about the world are internally related to the world. This almost goes without saying that truth is the logical feature of the sentences but this can be explained only in terms of the relation that the sentences have to the world. Hence the relation that we are talking about is logical and internal. The concept of satisfaction, by replacing the concept of fact, has paved the way for a better appraisal of the language-world relationship. At least, it has ruled out the fact that there is the possibility of a physicalistic[9] interpretation of the word-world relationship. Physicalism does not bear out the fact that truth as a formal relation partakes of any of the causal properties that are ascribable to language-world relationship.

Davidson is of the opinion that truth does not demand a fact-ontology.[10] It is because truth and facts are not the same thing. Facts are the entities that logicians and metaphysicians have introduced in order to define truth in terms of correspondence. But this requirement has been realized to be unwarranted as shown by Frege and Wittgenstein. Neither Frege nor Wittgenstein did see the importance of defining truth in terms of facts. Frege in fact did not have the concept of fact at all in his logical framework. Wittgenstein at best took it as a formal concept. Thus there is no reason why Davidson should fall for the facts in his truth theory. He, like Frege and Wittgenstein, takes it for granted that truth is an undefined and primitive concept in our logical system. Facts are thus abolished to make room for the objects and their properties that provide the satisfaction-conditions of the sentences concerned. This, however, does not mean that Davidson has no concept of the world which is the bedrock of all truth-characterizations. The world is ultimately that which language is all about.

For Davidson, truth brings language, world, man a ·d time together. That is to say, in his ontology, truth is the binding thread running from language to the world, that is, from man to language and then to the world in a temporal network. This is worked out in the following way. Man is the harbinger of language into the world and then man's entire relations to the world are structured through language. Thus language and the world are intimately related through man's actions and engagements with the world. But this takes place in the framework of time which makes language and actions woven in the network of time. Davidson highlights the fact that without time truth itself would not have been needed. Truth is the signal of the fact that language is engaged in the world and that man is busy representing the world in various ways. Unless the time-dimension is there, there is no reason why all sentences are not eternally true or eternally false. This will go against the possibility of representation of the world.

Davidson is of the view that truth is a relation among time, speaker and the world[11] in that whenever we assess the truth-value of a sentence we are bound to introduce the speaker, the temporal context and also the sector of the world about which the sentence is made. This is the way truth accrues to a sentence in language, e.g.'It is raining'. The time-indicator is so important in such sentences which use reflexive terms like 'it', etc. This is no small realization that truth is about what the speaker says, and that depends on what the world is. Here we need not say that the world makes the sentence true, for there is no way of knowing what the truth-value would have been if the world would not have been there.

Thus the theory of truth that Davidson proposes is meant for demonstrating that truth is the semantic concept that represents the logical structure of language. Besides, it aims at showing that truth is a pre-ontic notion that is embedded in language. In that sense truth does not depend on the ontological entities like facts and objects. Rather the concepts of fact and object themselves become meaningful because of the concept of truth. There is another dimension to truth which is generally not taken into account and that is its logical role in understanding language. Davidson shows that truth provides the method of interpreting language and meaning in such a way that meaning becomes definable in terms of the truth-conditions of the sentences. Language is thus intelligible in terms of the concept of truth. Thus we are brought back to the concept of representation as the important concept for Davidson. Though Rorty[12] feels that Davidson is a non-representationalist in his truth theory because he frees truth from the correspondence theory, it is yet admissible that for Davidson truth is anticipating representations in language since without them there is no necessity of truth in language at all. This is one of the reasons why we have started with the idea that the rationality of the discourse lies in the possibility of evaluating the linguistic representations of the world. Though Davidson does not say so, truth is the limit of our rationality and hence is so important to our entire linguistic effort to say what the world is.

Axioms of Truth and Meaning

Davidson seeks a solid structure for the truth theory for the reason that without such a structure truth cannot be finely situated in our conceptual scheme. Therefore he demands an axiomatized truth theory that lays down the basic laws of truth such as those governing the use of the predicate true in the context of the sentences. There are two such basic laws which are available for Davidson, namely,

1.   Convention T stating that a sentence S is true if and only if what the sentence says is the case. That is, schematically, S is true iff p.

where *S* is the name of a sentence and *p* is the sentence or its translation.

2. *T*-sentences which state the theorems concerning the extension of the concept of truth, that is, those sentences which follow from Convention *T*.

These two laws of truth are the basic laws because they lay down the axiomatic base for the operation of the concept of truth. Davidson takes a very serious account of these laws for the reason that, for him, truth operates in a formal way in the language-system. Following Tarski, he believes that truth obeys Convention *T* in that every truth-predication of sentences intuitively conforms to the schema given above. The truth-schema states that a sentence when called true does necessarily follow the principle given in 1. It is a necessary law that a sentence from natural language, e.g., "Snow is white" is true if and only if snow is white and not otherwise. This itself suggests that language and world being what they are it cannot be the case that the sentence "Snow is white" is true if and only if grass is green. Thus there is a logical necessity about the above *T*-schema. The second law states that, if all truth-sentences are available, that settles the issue whether truth is transparent in a language-system. That is to say that truth is a transparent predicate of sentences if there are *T*-sentences axiomatically following from Convention *T*. The latter is Davidson's special theory that so far as natural language is concerned *T*-sentences are axoimatically available, and that there is no gap between the intuitive understanding of truth and the axiomatic theory of it since truth is a primitive predicate of sentences and is available even at the less sophisticated level of the ordinary discourse.

Davidson's is an absolute theory of truth insofar as he does not attempt to define truth either in a Tarskian model-theoretic[13] way or in any other way that relativizes truth to the language in which it is defined. Both these options are ruled out because they take truth as a definable concept and that too in a language-dependent way. This possibility is not open for Davidson as this will entail that we go beyond language to define truth. Going beyond language is impossible as that demands a vantage point outside language. An absolute theory of truth inevitably follows as there is nothing outside language to contrast truth with.[14]

This theory of truth is generally called an extensional theory as there is the determinate sense in which truth is linked with the truth-conditions of sentences. The *T*-sentences are the extensional display of truth in language. This leads Davidson to say that the truth-conditions so displayed really carry the meaning of the sentences. Thus there is an inevitable relation between truth and meaning in this account. Truth being a more fundamental concept, it is inevitable that the meaning-structure of sentences is an extension of its truth-structure.[15] The following is the necessary law linking truth to meaning:

3.   The sentence *S* is meaningful if and only if the sentence has the truth-conditions laid in the corresponding *T*-sentence.

This law is extensional since there is no intensional notion of meaning taken for granted here. Meaning is the truth-conditions that are necessarily following from the *T*-sentences attached to the natural language sentences.

Davidson's account of meaning is novel in the sense that it frees the concept of meaning from the Fregean commitment to sense as an ontological entity. He makes meaning a definable and extensional concept in that, if a theory of truth is available, meaning is guaranteed without sacrificing the transparency attached to it. Like Quine, Davidson is aware that meaning is not an intensional entity that is to be located in a very queer way. His theory of meaning goes against the ideational as well as the referential account in that it does not presuppose that reference is an irreducible phenomenon. Reference goes inscrutable and, ultimately, is dropped from any semantic theory that takes truth as fundamental.[16]

The theory of meaning provides an account of our understanding of language as a whole and therefore there is no business for the semanticist to see what the words actually stand for. This is the demand of a holistic theory to which Davidson owes allegiance. A holistic theory says that the language as a whole needs a truth-strategy in terms of the intended interpretation of the sentences thereof. The truth-strategy is the one that has the intention to group all the sentences that can maximally be called true under the laws governing truth. The result is the interpretation of the sentences as true and meaningful across the linguistic groups to which we do not belong. Davidson here finds the necessity of an omniscient interpreter who can, across the board, interpret the sentences even of the distant native speakers of a tribe. Here what is needed is the Principle of Charity[17] that takes the interpreter above his or her parochial surroundings so as to understand the native speakers' utterances as true and meaningful. The native speaker's utterances are taken as true like ours and are consequently considered meaningful so far as they are speaking about the same world that we also talk about. Thus there is an agreement between the interpreter's community and the community of the native speakers such that truth remains the basic concept on which all agree. Meaning, apparently, may go indeterminate as in Quine's 'gavagai' case but, if truth is around, there is reason to believe that we may not ultimately fail to decipher meaning. Davidson is neither a meaning-sceptic nor a meaning indeterminist so far as his theory of meaning and interpretation is concerned.

What Davidson's theory of truth, meaning and interpretation achieves ultimately is the fact that language is an integrated system and that there is a single semantic network that goes to comprehend it in terms of truth. Thus there is the logic of truth that underlies all the sentences that are truth-relevant. This theory brings in the idea that what matters in language is its representational capacity and the ultimate capacity for truth. Davidson does not explain, nor does he need to, as to why sentences are representations and are truth-capable. Language, according to him, is representational in the sense that it is about reality in a very intimate sense. He agrees with Wittgenstein that there is no representation of the fact that language is representational since we cannot go beyond language to do it. We have to take an inside view of things and then declare that, if language is to be truth-predicable, then we must take for granted that there is the underlying need to see what language does in terms of its telling us about the world. The axiomatic theory of truth is the only response possible to the demand, as voiced by Rorty,[18] that truth go internal and immanent. By axiomatizing truth it is made impervious to the demands of relativism and subjectivism.

Truth, Reality and Representations

Davidson's axiomatic theory leads necessarily to a metaphysics[19] of truth insofar as truth is a method of understanding what the world is and shows what are the rational ways of understanding the meaning of the representations of the world. This is the thrust of the Davidsonain move to make truth a representational concept in that it applies only to sentences as they represent the world. Davidson dispenses with the scheme-content distinction because it proved to be a hindrance to the holistic theory that our conceptual scheme embedded in language is the one and the only one we have and so there is no meaning in saying that there are alternative conceptual schemes for us.[20] Those who talk of alternative schemes of thought do not take note of the fact that the conceptual schemes are not artificially designed and are not, for that matter, variable from person to person and from society to society. This being the case, there is no ground for saying that there are alternatives to how we think and represent the world. There is a single concept of truth and so there is a single conceptual scheme that we all inhabit. This looks, apparently, a hard-headed absolutism but there is no escape from the fact that, if a rational order of language and the world is possible, we cannot but treat our conceptual scheme as absolutely the unique one. This goes towards establishing the fact that a metaphysics of the world is possible even while offering a theory of truth.

The central theme of this metaphysics is that the world has a rational structure which can be represented in the structure of language. This is the main issue which the theory of truth for language highlights. Davidson has taken the rational order of language and the world as the foundation of his theory of truth. This is reflected in his idea that the truth-schema itself presents the rationality of the language-world relationship. Truth itself is the standard of rationality that philosophy can ever guarantee. So it is claimed by Davidson that the truth theory can explain how our statements about the world match the world in a perfect fit[21] so that there is no possibility of going wrong in the normal circumstances. This brings us back to the problem of the correspondence of the linguistic representations to the world so that we can see the way the world is found to be organized in the most rational way. Davidson, however, does not believe that the world can be organized[22] through the conceptual scheme we have in the way philosophers have suggested because this presupposes the scheme-content distinction which is otherwise outdated. That is to say, there is nothing like cutting the world into conceptual blocks for the rational ordering of it. This, in fact, is an empiricist myth created by the philosophers for making the world intelligible. What is of utmost importance is the fact that there is an intrinsic world-order that needs little rational justification. In that sense it becomes illusory to talk of rationalizing the world-order.

The truth theory makes the claim that the rational order of the world is only to be shown rather than justified. That is, the truth theory can alone demonstrate how the linguistic representations are capable of being true or false under the circumstances and not how the world is to be fitted into a given conceptual framework. The theory of truth reveals the truth-conditions of the sentences about the world and not how the truth-conditions are themselves possible. The latter requires a conceptual relativization of the world since, from outside of the conceptual scheme alone, can we see how the truth-conditions are possible. Davidson does not allow the possibility of conceptual relativism for the reason that there are no alternative conceptual frameworks possible. Disagreeing with the relativists Davidson argues that there is no reason why our conceptual scheme can be shown to be man-made and dependent on the socio-cultural factors.[23] The relativists argue that our conceptual schemes are all fabricated by us for organizing our experience of the world. So, for them, there is a possibility of having alternative schemes for the same purpose. Besides, they argue that there could be as many worlds as there are conceptual schemes.[24] This seems impossible for Davidson, as to have alternative conceptual schemes is to presuppose that there is one conceptual scheme within which alone these alternative schemes can be judged. This is very much reflected in our language which does not allow for alternative conceptions of truth as truth is the bedrock concept of all theories of language.

The challenge to truth theory and the underlying metaphysics that Davidson faces is not so much from relativism as from anti-realism and internal realism of Dummett and Putnam, respectively. Dummett claims that truth and world are both man-dependent to the extent the truth-conditions are really assertion-conditions given in a verifiable network of language. Thus there is reason to believe that the truth theory has no role to play in showing what the world is. It is at best a theory of conceptual construction[25] as it presents a world of our own making. Putnam tells, in a different way, that the world is dependent on our conceptual system and is internal to it in that, except within the system, we have no conception of the world as it is in itself.[26] This standpoint is a counterpoise to Davidson's as it says that there is no scope for having an absolute theory of truth at all as truth is a creature of our conceptual system and there is nothing substantial about it. Truth matters only as a rational criterion and has no absolute character about it. There can be different conceptions of truth as there are different conceptual systems. Davidson's rejoinder to this standpoint is that there is an absoluteness about our conceptual scheme and our concept of truth because that is the bedrock of our thinking. This theory need not be called realism as against anti-realism because this takes the absolute minimum to be the content of the theory of truth and the world. Like Frege and Wittgenstein, Davidson considers the concept of truth to be the minimum requirement of our thought and language and so there is no question of defining it or even justifying it in terms of something else.

The requirement of truth is the requirement of making the linguistic representations of the world intelligible. This is because, in the absence of the concept of truth, we do not know what to do with the representations we make regarding the world. That is to say, without a truth theory we may not have a theory of language at all. This makes Davidson internalize the concept of truth to the conceptual scheme itself, that is, to the language itself. Truth in that sense becomes a pre-analytic concept and operates within the semantic space without taking into account whether linguistic representations are themselves possible. In fact if truth is possible so are the representations of the world. There is thus a logical level that makes truth and representations co-present. It is not that first we have the concept of truth and then linguistic representations or *vice versa* but that we have them in the same semantic space. This is the crux of the Davidsonian argument that truth is a formal and internal feature of language and the linguistic representations. The reason is that the concept of language carries the notion of what it is that makes its claims about the world right or wrong. Certainly, the question is not whether the world makes them true or not but whether there is anything called making something true or not. The latter is the concept of truth that language internally possesses.

Truth is, for Davidson, the concept of judging whether we say something about the world rightly or wrongly. That is, it is the concept of making the language fit the world. Both language and the world face each other in the logical structure that is common to both and therefore the perfect fit between them is possible. This perfect fit is fully realized when we see the truth-schema displaying the truth-conditions. The perfect matching of the sentence and the world is shown in the metalanguage. The representational character of the sentence is shown in the matalanguage since in the object-language the sentence does its job without there being a manifest mechanism of representation. In fact there is no clear-cut notion of representation in any object-language. Both truth and representation are metalinguistic concepts and so they have the same logic.

This makes the truth theory of Tarski's a mere formal business as he has no concept of representation to explicate. Tarski is interested in the concept of truth as it is given in a formal language having no representational relation with the world. For him, truth can be formally displayed even if actually there is no world. A possible world is enough. But, for Davidson, the actual world and the actual language matter and what concerns him is the fact of their relationship. This is demonstrated in the metalanguage and the logic thereof. The latter does reflect the concern of language to represent the world. In fact logic is so called because it tells the exact representational character of the sentences. The first-order logic[27] is the logic of representations because the notion of quantifiers and truth-functions introduces the idea of representation. Davidson has made it the basis of the theory of representations that there must be the idea of quantification basic to it. The idea of truth-function is another logical concept that goes along with the concept of representation. Thus the concept of representation is implicit in the idea of formal logic presupposed by Davidson.

Davidson, however, has questioned the concept of reference which has dominated the theory of representation propounded by Russell and other empiricists except, of course, Quine. The classical idea of representation was tied down to the notion of reference where for every word some sort of reference was fixed. This was taken as a semantic requirement in view of the fact that words are meaningful only when they refer. But Quine questioned this hypothesis because of his belief that the sentences are the primary units of meaning and not the words themselves. This holistic approach has made Davidson argue that the reference of the words is inessential as the sentence is already in view with its truth-conditions. Theoretically speaking, we can dispense with the reference of the words because it is inscrutable[28] and also because we hardly need it. It is not that there are no objects in the world to be referred to but because this reference is not a semantic requirement at all. If language is internally representational, there is no other extra-linguistic mechanism to fix the reference of the words. In fact we cannot go beyond language to see which words refer to which objects in the world.

Davidson has gone beyond Quine in finding that language is a representational system. Since Quine was satisfied with the notion of linguistic behaviour and associated concept of meaning, he hardly bothered about the question whether language could be representational. He believed that linguistic responses constitute the content of all linguistic activities. But this is a gross simplification as language goes beyond these to talk about the world. Language is basically representing the world, though the representations are not always of the same type. The truth theory captures the nuances of the representations in their multifarious facets. This is, most of the time, forgotten in our enthusiasm to caricature language as a means of communication or a conventional system of linguistic responses to the environment. Davidson corrects this position by taking language as basically a system of representations which are capable of being true or false. If truth is foundational to a system of representations, then that must be the unique system of what we call language. Language is the system of what we say and also of what we do in relation to the world.

Interpretation, Belief and Meaning

The close ally of representational theory of language is the theory of interpretation provided by Davidson. Both together constitute the defence of representationality in the holistic framework. The theory of radical interpretation[29] as Davidson calls it is the theory of how we understand a language not necessarily our own that can be called true or false. This imposes on the interpreter the responsibility of understanding the truth or falsity of the sentences to be interpreted in the most rational manner. This requires the Principle of Charity and other logical considerations for taking the native speaker seriously. This entails the requirement of truth as the basic concept in all languages, whether our own or other's. This is the special feature of interpretation that we place ourselves in the place of the speaker whom we are interpreting. Here the speaker is taken as one of us and thereby we try to understand what he says. Since the speaker is talking about the world and he is talking in the manner amenable to logic, the interpreter manages a good deal to find out whether he is speaking truly or falsely. It is not factually the case that the speaker's utterances are all false and there is nothing for the interpreter to do about it. Such a situation does not arise because the speaker happens to be a truth-speaker and he is as much rational as we are. We have the responsibility of interpreting charitably and rationally.

Now the question arises as to the relation of interpretation to representationality of language. It is taken for granted that truth is the basis of interpretation and it is also the basis of linguistic representations. So on this count interpretations and representations converge on truth. Besides, truth is the truth of representations and therefore there is nothing else that can be true or false. In this sense, whenever we have to understand the meaning of any sentence, we have to see whether it is true or not. We cannot bypass truth to decipher the meaning because though we understand the meaning of a sentence even before knowing whether it is true, we cannot understand how it can be meaningful without being either true or false. That is, we cannot understand the meaning of the sentence without understanding the truth-conditions thereof. Thus interpretation is logically bound up with the truth-conditions of the sentential representations. Thus we can see that the theory of representations and the theory of interpretation meet on the theory of truth.

The question of meaning is not bypassed for that matter nor is it rejected out of hand. Davidson takes meaning to be nested in the representations in the sense that meaning is basically a feature of the representations. But, whereas truth is pre-analytically taken, meaning is not so taken. So meaning has to be introduced through the truth-conditions of the representations. Here therefore the question of beliefs and their relation to meaning arises. Meaning meshes with beliefs because the latter are the contents of all representations. Beliefs are the content of all representations since they are believed to be true or false regarding the world. A belief system is as much in need of the truth-conditions as are the representations and so there are via media of beliefs to reach the meaning of the representations. Davidson has shown this in his theory that underlying any system of representations there is a system of beliefs. The latter matters as the source of meaning. Meaning will not be possible if the assertions made in language are also not believed and accepted. Besides, they must be believed as a whole and not piecemeal. Hence the need for a holistic theory of meaning.

The evidence for holism lies in the fact that beliefs are interlocked in a network such that there is no way of separating one from the other. Since beliefs and assertions go together it is inevitable that there is a system in which they are situated. This system is the language which the theory of interpretation takes as its subject-matter. As Davidson has made clear, it is impossible to understand the meaning of a language without taking the belief-system into account. It is because to interpret is to ascribe beliefs to the speaker and thus to get at what he intends to express. This, of course, involves the risk of not finding the exact meaning of the speaker's utterances under the circumstances. That is, there is the possibility of indeterminacy of meaning even when the network of beliefs is presupposed. Davidson, however, takes this possibility in his stride, unlike Quine, because he believes that there is a way of minimizing the indeterminacy in the overall scheme of interpretation. The aim of the interpretation theory is to maximize[30] the agreement between the interpreter and the speaker whose utterances are being interpreted.

Given that interpretation involves maximum agreement on beliefs and their truth-conditions, there is the important problem of relating the beliefs to the world which provides the background for these truth-conditions. Davidson keeps this in mind while considering the nature of the truth-conditions themselves. Since meaning, for him, is the other face of the truth-conditions, there is no extra entity called meaning to explain how the world is logically involved in language. That is why we have to search for the representational content in meaning in the truth-conditions of the sentences. In fact the truth-conditions as displayed in the T-sentences are the representation-conditions which are presented in the R-(representation)-sentences. We can call a T-sentence a R-sentence meaning thereby that each such sentence gives the conditions under which a sentence can be taken as true or false. The R-sentence can be formulated as follows:

4. "Snow is white" is R-true iff snow is white.

This sentence captures the same conditions as the corresponding *T*-sentence such that where the latter is meaningful the former is equally meaningful. Thus there is a logical link between the truth-conditions and the representation-conditions.

Davidson, like Tarski, is concerned with the logical features which constrain the truth of a sentence but he goes further in searching for the constraints imposed by the world on these logical features. The latter constraints are such as are found in the fact that the world alone determines whether the *R*-conditions are fulfilled or not. The satisfaction of these conditions is absolutely necessary for there to be linguistic representations at all. The conceptual scheme itself is not enough to vouchsafe for the truth- and representation-conditions of the sentences. It can, at best, provide the logical structure of the *R*-sentence in the metalanguage but that is not enough. There must be empirical constraints on the *R*-sentences themselves.

Davidson, in his theory of truth and interpretation, has kept room for the notion of representation to the extent it helps him in keeping the language-world relationship intact. Davidson's worry is to make the world transparent in language, as Frege and Wittgenstein also tried to do before him. But where Frege took the help of logic to do it and Wittgenstein appealed only to the fact of language-use, Davidson went in search of a theory of truth and interpretation to provide for the representation-relation between language and the world. This theory has the advantage that it keeps the problem at the top of the semantic agenda and makes elaborate effort to make the world visible in the very activity of speaking and also in understanding the speech of others. The semantic holism that follows is the doctrine of relating the speech of all participants in the community-activity of using language under the constraints of truth and rationality. Thus there arises the need of an integral theory of language, actions and the life of the community.

Semantic Holism and the Constraints of Empiricism

Davidson's semantic system goes holistic in view of the need of language to be a system of speech, beliefs and conventions for communication. And, above all that, there is the underlying need of a system of logic of truth-conditions. But does this augur well for semantics as such? Is holism itself wholesome? This will be the theme of the rest of the chapter as Dummett has challenged holism in his theory of meaning in recent times.

Before we encounter the anti-holist, let us see if Davidson himself has followed the logic of holism fully. It appears that he is in favour of a universal system of truth and interpretation that can make an across-the-board use of the concept of truth. Besides, it also appears that he favours the idea of a rational system of rules for understanding any language whatever. All these are the assumptions of a holistic theory of language and meaning. But Davidson's Quinean background holds him committed to empiricism to the extent of justifying the truth theory itself in experience. This may result in accepting a gap between what is true in language and what is actually the case in the world. This may further lead to the view that there is indeterminacy in the meaning of the sentences for which we can offer truth-conditions. All these are admitted in the holistic system with the proviso that there is a chance for a universal system of understanding of language. It, of course, does not mean that there is a common language[31] to provide universal conditions of agreement. Davidson does not recognize the idea that there is a universal language that holds all mankind in the unique bond of truth-speaking. As an empiricist, for him, there are many languages and many systems of rules and conventions. Therefore there is a pluralistic semantic situation that requires the theory of interpretation to cement the differences amongst the linguistic communities.

Thus semantic holism is not universalism[32] nor is it semantic determinism. It is an open-ended theory that relies on the possibility of multiple linguistic phenomena. But it claims that, in spite of differences, there is the possibility of their coming under the theory of interpretation and truth. The claim of the opponents of holism is that truth is not a universal concept that can provide for a unification of all the languages under a single semantic system. According to them, if there are many languages there must be many semantic theories and there is nothing like a single theory of truth and interpretation. If this view is correct, then there cannot be any scientific view of the world since our experiences are many and our articulations diverse. That is, we cannot have a unified view of the experiences we have and cannot get over the impending subjectivism and solipsism. This, in fact, if extended into semantics, will mean we cannot understand each other and there cannot be anything called common understanding. This is averted by Davidson by saying that truth is a universal concept though there may be many ways of understanding it. Universality of truth does not mean universality of language, and besides, there is nothing like having one's own truth and meaning. Davidson follows Wittgenstein in rejecting the private idiolects and languages that threaten the very language and conceptual scheme we have.

The real threat to holism comes from empiricism itself. With the fall of the scheme-content distinction there is a fresh challenge from the Quinean indeterminists that truth, like meaning, must become language-relative and so we can have as many truth theories as there are conceptual systems. This follows the lead of the relativists who have no conception of an absolute theory of truth. But, as argued earlier, the possibility of different conceptual schemes is itself a self-defeating notion and therefore must be rejected.

Holism further meets with the challenge that it cannot tell how language is a system and how the system itself works. If the languages are systems, how can we make intelligible the idea that we can learn the language? Dummett's argument is that languages are basically learnt[33] and there is nothing like learning the whole language. So we must see language as a molecular structure with multiple storeys so that we can situate a sentence at a particular place in the structure and can have a mastery of that sentence under given grammatical conventions. As we shall further elaborate later, this argument does not threaten holism as the latter never denies that we learn the language piecemeal. Language is like a system from the point of view of grammar and that shows that there is nothing to hinder learning of the language by mastery of words and sentences in a piecemeal fashion. But once the learner has a full view of the language, he can understand it only as one whole.

Empiricism cannot overcome the scheme-content distinction fully and so there is a vestigial form of indeterminism in the semantic theory of truth. This could be overcome only if language is detached from the empirical view of the world. The nature of world must be taken in the logical sense and so there could be a fresh way of undertaking the investigation of the language-world relationship. This could be done if there is a comeback to the root of modern semantics, that is, the Fregean notion of sense. Dummett provides the promise in his theory of meaning which we shall consider now. Our effort will be to see if Dummett has a better theory˙ of language-world relationship and a more adequate theory of representation.

Dummett and the Semantics of Assertions

Dummett's semantics is one of determining the meaning of the assertions in language rather than of truth or the truth-conditions. His aim is to fix the assertion-conditions of the sentences in the network of the linguistic use. So he finds that semantics of the truth-conditions so far pursued has not yielded the proper insight into the nature of meaning.[34] The classical theory of truth which is presupposed by the semantics of truth-conditions has been challenged by Dummett for it has failed to lead us to the proper theory of meaning.

Dummett begins his inquiry into the nature of language and meaning by examining the classical realist[35] notion of truth. According to him, the notion of truth in classical logic needs a thorough re-examination as it has given a very narrow view of language. For the classical logic, the only language available is the one of sentences in the indicative mood. That is to say, classical logic presents a picture of language that consists of assertions and their truth-conditions. This is the language presupposed in the logical systems of Frege, Russell and Wittgenstein in the *Tractatus*. The hallmark of such a view of language is that it presents a static view of language and the world. For it what matters is the impersonal logical structure of language without taking the language-user into account. This results, as Dummett, following the later Wittgenstein, realizes, in the narrowing down of language into the one of sentences which are the representations of the world in the logical sense. This point of view not only neglects the language-user but also the dimension of time involved in language-use. The resulting realism about truth, meaning and the world is the stumbling block to the understanding of language in the proper perspective.

Dummett introduces two categories for correcting the realist picture of language and the world, namely, (1) the user and time axes of language and (2) the dynamic structure of the world that is not indifferent to the perceiver. The first category tells us that the assertions that we make in language and which logic takes as impersonal pieces of language are really soaked in time and are the results of the user's intention to speak something. Thus the linguistic assertions are not merely linguistic pieces but also are the statements made by people. Therefore for judging the truth-value of the assertions we must take into account the assertion-conditions of the statements. The truth of the assertions is not decidable independently of the these conditions as it is not the case that the assertions are timeless entities in a grammatical domain. That is the reason Dummett brings in the notion of a dynamic world in a temporal continuum that makes it easier to recognize that the world is very much responsive to the perceiver and language-user.

Dummett calls his new perspective anti-realism which means that it does not take for granted that there is a truth which is independent of the language-user, nor is there a world that is independent of the activity of representing it in language. Thus anti-realism makes an important move in semantics and metaphysics. In semantics it lays down that the principle of bivalence[36] of the classical logic does not hold good because truth cannot be decided independently of the language-user. That is, the idea that a sentence is either true or false logically does not hold good since we do not know what the truth of a sentence is without the assertion-conditions themselves. Dummett calls the realist notion of truth cognition-transcendent[37] as it goes beyond the cognitive capacity of the statement-maker. Thus the anti-realist picture of language and truth suggests that truth is internal to the cognitive mechanism of the language-user. This has the added result that nothing matters in semantics other than the assertion-conditions of the sentences and their temporal character.

In metaphysics the anti-realist conception of the world emerges replacing the static universe of the realists. Dummett underlines the fact that what is called the world is not a finished entity in the way Frege might have suggested. It has the character of becoming in time and therefore there is the world of empirical objects that can be taken as growing in course of our discovery. Thus in metaphysics what matters is the world perceived and known, and there is nothing like the world given independently of the knower. The world is no less a matter of our making, that is, our invention. Taking the parallel from mathematics, Dummett tells us that mathematical objects are not a matter of discovery at all. They are the inventions of the mathematicians as much as without our activity of doing mathematics they are not available in language at all. The anti-realist view of mathematics is called intuitionism or constructivism[38] that promises that there is nothing independent of the cognizer in any domain of cognition.

Dummett thus holds, both in semantics and metaphysics, that the basic notion of truth in language must be restated in terms of the conditions under which assertions are made. It is the language that is the basic notion in semantics and metaphysics. By understanding language alone, we can tell what truth and meaning are and what the world actually is. Thus, according to Dummett, philosophy of language is the foundation of metaphysics and other disciplines like philosophy of mathematics.

Truth, Meaning and Representations

Dummett's main thesis is: the theory of meaning must be built on the basis of the new anti-realist picture of language and the world. The theory of meaning must tell what constitutes the conditions under which we call a sentence meaningful. That is to say, a theory of meaning must be a theory of understanding[39] of language as such. A theory of meaning must take care to tell how the language-users develop semantic competence to correctly use language under the appropriate conditions. This leads to what Dummett calls the language-mastery that manifests the linguistic abilities which a competent user of language must possess. Thus the meaning theory includes a theory of linguistic competence.

The other important feature of meaning theory is that it does not accept the Fregean concept of cognition-independent sense that has nothing to do with the linguistic practice. Dummett recognizes that without the practice there is no essence of language that manifests the sense embedded in language.

Language is the language-game or the language-practice and therefore sense or meaning must be the one we recognize in the ongoing business of language. There are two ways we can understand the nature of meaning. The first way is the usual one where we take for granted that meaning is the truth-conditions of the sentences if they make assertions about the world. This Dummett calls the realist theory of meaning espoused by Frege and the early Wittgenstein. The other way is the one where meaning is a matter of linguistic practice, that is, where meaning is a matter of use and practice. The latter theory does not presuppose that meaning is independent of the cognition of the language-user.

The following are the two theses of the anti-realist theory of meaning:

1. Meaning is a matter of language-use and therefore is immanent to language. The language-user fully controls the mechanism of the meaning theory as a competent speaker of the language.

2. Meaning is not a matter of truth-conditions since the latter are not given to our cognitive mechanism. Truth is not the basis of meaning though it is the other way round. That is, meaning is the basis of truth and falsity.

The first thesis is the positive thesis that tells that a meaning theory need not search for meaning anywhere else than in the language-use. That is to say, we can decipher the meaning in the practical method of verifying whether a statement is true or false. This leads to a sort of verificationism[40] that leaves no gap between what is asserted meaningfully and the assertion being true or false. The second thesis tells that there is no way to meaning via truth as the latter concept has still the stigma of being beyond our cognition. Truth as such is a concept of evaluating the sentences in the context of the world. But, before the evaluation takes place, there must already be meaning in the sentences and so it cannot be case the that meaning itself depends upon truth. In view of this, Dummett recognizes that meaning is pre-conceptual and linguistic in character. By its being pre-conceptual is meant that it is not the result of a definite procedure followed for understanding language. Meaning is the understanding of language itself and so there is nothing conceptual before language is understood. Thus there is a definite way of understanding meaning by using language.

Dummett does not reject the Fregean concept of sense completely. Rather, he brings about a revision in the notion of sense. For Frege, sense is transcendent to our cognitive grasp and so it is posited in the transcendent realm of logic. Thus there arises a gap between the thought or sense and the linguistic expressions of it. Dummett dissolves the gap and in its place keeps the sense-content as the linguistic content of all assertions. Sense is now the content of assertions and is amenable to verificationist constraints. The immanent nature of sense does not rule out its normative nature nor does it weaken its logical status. Sense is still the meaning-structure of the assertions and there is nothing hidden about it. This makes meaning a full-blooded concept and is robustly present in the linguistic mechanism itself.

Like Frege's sense, Dummett's sense is also representational in that it is the thought-content of the assertions. The assertions are about the world and are either true or false depending upon what the world is. Thus the basic structure of the assertion is its representational character. It is a way of telling what the world is. Though this is not the only way of language-use, it is the most fundamental way. So there is reason to believe that truth is one of the ways in which the assertion can be made. Keeping this in mind we can say that the sense of the true or false assertions must be representational. Dummett tells us that language is keeping itself abreast of the world in our daily life and so it becomes imperative that the world is presented to us by language in the mechanism of language-use. The representationality of sense lies in the fact that meaning itself cannot be understood except within the framework of our representation of the world.

Dummett's semantics presents the model of a constructivist theory of truth and meaning. Both truth and meaning are subject to the decisions of the people using language. This is called the mind-dependency of the semantic concepts. This leads further to the idea that in order to know the truth of a sentence we must be able to decide under what conditions it is true. This latter condition underlines the need for what Dummett calls the finite decidability of truth.[41] This need is the semantic necessity of grounding sentences in a finite time-frame such that truth is no more a cognition-transcendent concept. So now there is no requirement of defining truth-conditions in a use-independent way. In fact, for Dummett, truth and use must go together in the sense that, without the effective use of a sentence, there cannot be any decision as to when the truth can be known to the user of the sentence. In this sense an anti-realist semantics also can accommodate truth if the sufficient decidability conditions are fulfilled.[42]

Now the question arises, how does Dummett face the challenge of the realist who refuses to dispense with the concept of truth in favour of the concept of assertability-conditions of a sentence? The realist feels that any theory of language and truth must take truth as a fundamental concept and so there is no question of truth being anyway transcendent to the cognitive mechanism of the language-user. To this Dummett's reply is that truth is as such not a transcendent concept but the realist theory of truth makes it so. So there is the anti-realist demand for making truth available verificationally in our cognitive repertoire. The demand is for verification and not for the displacement of the concept of truth. This is the heart of the anti-realist semantics that calls for a revision of the classical notion of truth. The fact of the matter is that truth and meaning both are subject to the finite decidability conditions and those conditions are fulfilled only in a verificational use-semantics. Dummett has very aptly called it the theory of meaning rather than of truth since for him truth is not so important as meaning.

From our point of view, Dummett's theory of meaning is representational as it has not ruled out the possibility of truth being a representational concept. Besides, he has not rejected the view that meaning is itself a concept related to the fact of saying something about the world. The saying is representing in that, through that mechanism alone, there is the possibility of saying something true or false. The theory of representation that we are pursuing is the one that keeps room for the concept of truth and also accommodates a full-blooded sense of the notion of sense. Sense is the ground-level semantic reality that can hardly be rejected in the name of anti-realism. In fact Dummett is concerned to keep sense as the basic component of a theory of meaning along with a theory of force such that language is taken as a system of meaningful representations in their various facets of use, i.e., the speech-acts. The concept of representation is thus basic to Dummett's semantics.

Dummett Against Holism

Dummett, as already indicated, faces holism squarely in his theory of meaning and representation. He is against holism precisely because he feels that the latter leads to realism and that it does not explain how the truth-conditions of the sentences are known to the language-user. The argument that Dummett provides takes it for granted that truth is basic to holism, as in Davidson, and the truth theory is the foundation of the holistic theory of language. But this seems wrong as neither Davidson nor any other holist thinks that truth is the only concept on which holism stands. Though it is true that truth is a fundamental concept for Davidson it is not the case that he chooses it as a matter of policy. It is thrust upon the semanticist as the indefinable concept and so there is no metaphysical motive behind the concept of truth. It is therefore unreasonable to believe that truth leads to realism. In fact realism is a metaphysical doctrine that needs truth to prove that there is a world independently of our mind. This is the result of assuming that truth and the world are correlated in the correspondence way. But Davidson, like Frege, rejects the classical correspondence theory of truth.

The real challenge is the one that holds that holism does not allow language-mastery in the sense that one cannot learn the whole of a language at a time. This really points to a psychological impossibility rather than to a logical impossibility. Human beings are not capable of learning the whole language because the latter has infinite sentences built out of a finite vocabulary. But this does not rule out the fact that when a child learns a language it learns the language as such, not a part of it. There is nothing like learning a part of a language. Language is either a whole or it is nothing. Thus holism is hard to be defeated when the empirical evidences support the holistic character of language.

The fact remains that language-mastery is not a piecemeal affair. It is a process of internalizing the semantic rules and manifesting the competence in the language-use. Dummett very rightly recognizes that semantic competence is the implicit knowledge that we have for understanding the language. However, there is no reason to believe that language can be mastered only piecemeal. Language-mastery is as much holistic as language itself.

Anti-realism cannot really show that language is not representational. Even if intuitive construction of reality is allowed for, as in mathematics, there is no way of telling that this can be done independently of language itself. The construction has to be in the language and there must be a grammatical justification for that. So there cannot be an arbitrary way of making the reality in the idealist sense. Dummett realizes the limits of constructing the external reality so much so that he really rejects the idea that reality is subjective in the crude sense. Reality is, at best, a semantically intelligible world that is given to our epistemological framework. Language is still the basic framework in which the reality is presented to us. Thus there cannot be any escape from the fact that language is representational and that all our links with the world are structured through language.

The anti-realist semantics has the promise to bring out a better understanding of the language-world relationship since, for it, the world is no more an alien and mind-independent stuff. In fact here the world is a constant presence in the network of language so much so that the moment we speak we encounter the world in its various facets. This is the Kantian requirement that the reality as it is given in experience is the one fully structured through the categories. That we cannot make much of the concept of a language-transcendent world is obvious in the writings of the so-called realists such as Davidson and the early Wittgenstein. The later Wittgenstein, like Kant, has echoed the above demand that language and the world are so related that there is no way of telling what the world is independently of language. If this is the main thesis of anti-realism, then there is no reason to believe that anti-realism has given up representationalism.

The chief difficulty in Dummett's theory is not anti-realism but his molecular theory of language which leads to the conception that language consists of a multistoreyed structure.[43] This view of language falsifies the real nature of language because it tells as if there is a definite formal way in which language can be constructed. Really speaking, language is a mass phenomenon that makes little room for hierarchy. That is, there is a single system that presents the multifaceted character of language.

Language has many facets but not many levels. The level theory is a misrepresentation of language.

The other difficulty is his verificationism.[44] Though verificationism is partially true it is not the case that language has to be verificational throughout. There are features of language that are understood without looking into the world. The poetic utterances are not verified in the world, not because they have nothing to do with the world, but because there is no way of verifying them. So also large part of our language is non-verificational. Meaning is not a method of verification at all as before verifying anything we must be assured of its meaning.

To conclude: the theory of representation is well entrenched in the semantic theories of Davidson and Dummett. The aim of this chapter is to prove that representationality, being a basic notion, is not threatened by the realist-anti-realist controversy. The status of truth is not the issue because truth is so fundamental to our conceptual scheme that both realism and anti-realism presuppose it. Their differences are an internal matter to semantics since both agree that language is basically representational.

References

1.   *See* Dummett, *Frege: Philosophy of Language* (Duckworth, London,1973).

2.   Cf. Wittgenstein, *Philosophical Investigations*,tr. by G.E.M. Anscombe (Blackwell,Oxford, 1953).

3.   The notion of immanent grammar is Quine's. *See his* Philosophy *of Logic* (Prentice-Hall, Inc., Englewood Cliffs, N.J.,1970).

4.   Cf. W.V. Quine, "Two Dogmas of Empiricism", in *From a Logical Point of View* (Harvard University Press, Cambridge, Massachusetts, 1953).

5.   A. Tarski, "The Concept of Truth in Formalized Languages", in *Logic, Semantics, Metamathematics* (Clarendon Press,Oxford, 1956).

6. Cf. Donald Davidson, "Truth and Meaning", in *Inquiries into Truth and Interpretation* (Clarendon Press, Oxford, 1984).

7. **See** Hintikka and Hintikka, *Investigating Wittgenstein* (Blackwell, Oxford, 1986) for the concept of language as a universal medium. This concept has important implications for understanding logical semantics.

8. **See** Tarski, "The Concept of Truth in formalized Languages".

9. **See** H. Field, "Tarski's Theory of Truth", in *Reference, Truth and Reality*, ed. by Mark Platts (Routledge and Kegan Paul, London,1980).

10. For the conception of fact-ontology, **see** Wittgenstein, *Tractatus Logico-Philosophicus* tr. by D. F. Pears and B. F. McGuinness (Routledge and Kegan Paul, London, 1961). For Davidson's critique of this ontology **see his** "True to the Facts", in *Inquiries into Truth and Interpretation.*

11. Cf. Davidson, "Truth and Meaning".

12. Richard Rorty, "Representation, Social Practise and Truth", in *Objectivism, Relativism and Truth* (Cambridge University Press, Cambridge,1991).

13. Cf. "The Concept of Truth in Formalized Languages".

14. **See** Davidson, "In Defence of Convention T", in *Inquiries into Truth and Interpretation.*

15. *Ibid.* **See also** Davidson, "Truth and Meaning".

16. For the inscrutability of reference thesis, **see** Davidson, "The Inscrutability of Reference", in *Inquiries into Truth and Interpretation.*

17. **See** Davidson, "Thought and Talk", in *Inquiries into Truth and Interpretation.*

18. **See** Rorty, *Objectivism, Relativism and Truth.*

19. For the metaphysical implications of the theory of truth, **see** Davidson, "The Method of Truth in Metaphysics", in *Inquiries into Truth and Interpretation.*

20. Cf. Davidson, "On the Very Idea of a Conceptual Scheme", in *Inquiries into Truth and Interpretation.*

21. *Ibid.*

22. *Ibid.*

23. *Ibid.*

24. *Ibid.*

25. For Dummett's criticism of the holistic theory of meaning, **see** his "What is a Theory of Meaning?", in *Mind and Language*, ed. by S. Guttenplan (Clarendon Press, Oxford,1975).

26. **See** Hilary Putnam, *Meaning and Moral Sciences* (Routledge and Kegan Paul, London, 1978).

27. **See** Davidson, "Semantics of Natural Languages", in *Inquiries into Truth and Interpretation.*

28. Cf. Davidson, "The Inscrutability of Reference".

29. Cf. Davidson, "Radical Interpretation", in *Inquiries into Truth and Interpretation.*

30. *Ibid.*

31. On the issue of a common language, **see** Davidson, "A Nice Derangement of Epitaphs", in *Truth and Interpretation*, ed. by E. LePore (Blackwell, Oxford,1989). For further discussion on this issue, **see** B. T. Ramberg, *Donald Davidson's Philosophy of Language* (Blackwell,Oxford,1989).

32. For the criticism of Davidson on the possibility of a universal language, **see** Ian Hacking, "The Parody of Conversation",in *Truth and Interpretation*, ed. by E. LePore. **See also** Dummett, "A Nice Derangement of Epitaphs: Some Comments on Davidson and Hacking", in *Truth and Inetrpretation.*

33. **See** Dummett,"What is a Theory of Meaning?".

34. *Ibid.*

35. **See** Dummett, "Truth", in *Philosophical Logic*, ed. by P.F. Strawson (Oxford University Press, Oxford,1967).

36. *Ibid.*

37. *Ibid.*

38. **See** Dummett, "What is a Theory of Meaning? II", in *Truth and Meaning*, ed. by G. Evans and J. McDowell (Oxford University Press,Oxford,1976).

39.   *Ibid.*

40.   *Ibid.*

41.   *Ibid.*

42.   **See** C. McGinn, "Truth and Use", in *Reference, Truth and Reality,* ed. by M. Platts.

43.   Cf. Dummett, "What is a Theory of Truth? II".

44.   *Ibid.*

4

Truth, Reference and the World-Order

IN our understanding of the structure of representations in chapters 2 and 3 we have already foreshadowed the problem of the world-order. We have been reminded of the imperative character of the problem of the world for the philosophers of language in view of the fact that language is the representation of the world and that in language alone we have the world presented in its multifarious character. So the problem that stares us in the face is: What world-order do we represent in language? And how can truth (and meaning) make a dent in that order? Obviously the world-order is not a matter of empirical revelation nor is it a matter of intuitive grasp independently of language. Therefore we are bound to come back to the semantic framework of our language to understand the world-order. Neither experience nor intuition is capable of revealing the reality without the help of language. So the philosopher of language looks to language to find out the logical order of the universe.

Now the question is: What is the order that semantics reveals? This has puzzled philosophers throughout the centuries. One thing which the philosophers have recognized as vital is that language reveals the logical form[1] or order of the world rather than the contingent details of the factual world-order. It is not that language does not state what objects are there in the world, but that, logically speaking, the order of the world is more prominently displayed in the structure of language. Philosophy is interested in the logical form or order of the world because it is this form alone that provides the clue to the understanding of the universe.

Traditionally, philosophers have been struggling with the problem of thought and being since they believed that there is an essential unity of the two which can be captured in philosophical reflections. This made Hegel argue that, in philosophical reflection, there is the realization of the unity of thought and reality. This principle of the unity of thought and being has been the cornerstone of classical metaphysics. It is no wonder that linguistic philosophy has not been completely freed from this problem in spite of its largely anti-metaphysical character. The reason is that the problem of thought and being is as basic as logic and language and that to think in and about language is to be involved in the idea of being itself. Language is the home of being, as Heidegger[2] has declared, and there is reason to believe that linguistic philosophy largely believes that language and being are inseparable and uniquely related.

In this chapter, I shall present the semantic argument for the possibility of the logical world-order or the being and try to show that the concepts of truth and meaning go a long way towards establishing that the world-order is the foundation of the very possibility of linguistic representations. Reality or the being is not only linguistically represented but also is indexed in the very structure of truth and meaning.

Truth-Based Semantics

Truth-based semantics provides the framework for the understanding of the world-order, as it is within this framework that reality can be studied in its logical aspects. As indicated earlier, the structure of language shows the structure of the world in a non-defeasible manner. The following are the two important features of truth-based semantics which are relevant in this regard:

(a)   The theory of reference that pins down the referring expressions to the objects in the world.

(b)   The theory of sentence that makes the linguistic representations the vehicles of truth.

In (a) we have the principle of objectual reference which is the dominant concern of the truth-based semantics. Objectual reference, as Frege has characterized it, is the foundation of the theory of predication and quantification. That is, the idea of predication entirely depends on the availability of the idea of objectual reference. So there is a canonical way of regimenting reference in the semantic discourse. Quine's celebrated dictum "To be is to be the value of a variable" is the required principle of the semantic discourse that ensures that reference is built into the canons of truth-based semantics.

But (a) is incomplete without the other principle embodied in (b) which is, in fact, the law of truth. According to this law, the sentences are the vehicles of truth, that is, are those which alone are characterizable as true or false. This principle is important in view of the fact that even the principle of reference cannot work unless there is a sentential structure wherein the referring expressions have a function. Frege's well-known context principle is precisely the one that has shown that the sentence is the primary linguistic unit of meaning or sense.[3] This principle is basic to much of truth-based semantics as the sentential primacy has been increasingly realized to be the core of linguistic representations.

Now let us see why truth and reference are allied symbiotically in semantics in spite of the fact that Quine and Davidson have cast doubt on the indispensability of reference itself. It is, nonetheless, the case that without reference the idea of truth may not work at all. In fact truth is an index of the normality of reference in our discourse. Truth cannot be ascribed to the sentences if reference itself is aborted. However, it is true that, in a holistic framework, reference can be taken care of internally and therefore without much logically hassle.

Let us take the following sentence which is not semantically normal since it aborts its reference:

* The present king of India is the wisest man in the world.

This sentence holds the reference a hostage as it does not find out which man in the world is the wisest man. As Russell[4] has shown in his theory of descriptions, this sentence does not fulfil the existential condition and so its reference is completely aborted. Here what is to be noticed is that the sentence in spite of its syntactic normality is not semantically cogent as it incurs a reference-failure. The reference-failure[5] is the index of the fact that the sentence cannot be called true or false under the circumstance that the sentence is not making any referential ascription to any particular individual. Thus we can make the claim that, as long as reference has not been completely secured, there is no truth-possibility at all. The truth of the starred sentence above is nowhere in the horizon. Following Frege, we shall call this semantic situation the situation of truth-value gap such that, whenever there is aborted reference, there is the lack of truth-value in the sentence.

The situation of reference-failure is the one of the sentence going out of the normal semantic discourse since it indicates that there is something seriously missing in the sentence. What is missing is the normal semantic cogency of the sentence. In fact, nothing has been said in the sentence except the fact that an empty expression has been used for no semantic purpose. The sentences thus going semantically abnormal are to be bracketed in the semantic discourse so that we keep as closely as possible to the principle of reference.

The principle of reference lays down two types of semantic link between language and the world. The first type of link is the objectual link that runs from the word to the object. This link is guaranteed by the sentence itself. This link we may call the forward-looking link between the words and their objectual counterparts. The other type of link is the one between sentence and the world. Here there is no objectual link except the projection relations between the sentence and the world. The world is the other side of the projection of which the sentences constitute the linguistic side. As Wittgenstein's *Tractatus*[6] has shown, there are really no two sets of relation between word and object, and between sentence and the world. In fact they make an integral whole in which the sentence stands guarantee for the word-object link. In such a system there cannot be a contingent non-linguistic link between words and the objects, or, for that matter, there is no extra-linguistic way of telling what the words stand for. It is the sentence alone which tells how the words function within it so far as their reference is concerned.

The words in the sentences constitute a new set of relationships to be semantically taken note of. These relationships are inward-looking and are logically to be constituted. They are to be settled as we go on telling how the sentences have their sense in the context of the language-world relationships. The first thing that comes to our notice is the fact that sentences form a unity in their logical structure such that there is a holistic framework for understanding the place of the words in the sentence. That is to say, the sentences are integral structures that have to be taken as single entities.[7] In view of this, the words have to be taken as dependent on the sentences such that we can no more say that words are themselves meaningful independently of the sentence.

Frege has settled this issue between words and the sentences in favour of the sentences but he did not go the whole way towards establishing the holistic theory which was brought to light by Wittgenstein. The latter theory has made it clear that sentences are semantically primary and are the vehicles of truth and meaning. In this framework the words are not unimportant but are nonetheless dependent on the sentence. This theory affects the overall picture of semantics because there is no more the effort to situate reference outside the sentential structure. The classical theories of reference are inadequate because they have no way to tell how the word-reference is possible without the sentence already having a meaning. If therefore sense is guaranteed to the sentences before the word-reference is settled, then there is no reason to believe that truth-based semantics needs a principle of reference. There is in Frege a tension between the word-reference and the sentence-sense and it can be resolved either by taking recourse to holism such that the reference principle is integrated into the principle of truth and sense, or word-reference goes the causal way such that the principle of reference leads to a causal theory of reference.[8] The latter has been accepted by those who are dissatisfied with Frege's solution to the problem of reference. The dominant concern in this chapter is to show that the holistic account might have a chance in resolving the Fregean dilemma.

Sense and the World

The Fregean theory of sense has the potentiality of showing how the sentence-sense is the semantic reality that can stand the test against the causal theorists. Causal theorists hold that sense of a sentence is only an accidental feature because, in causally tracing the roots of reference, the sense that we attach to the linguistic expressions is a matter of convention and that the resulting sense is a minimal thing that is associated with the reference mechanism. They refute the Fregean theory that sense determines reference. According to them, the causal history of a name or referring expression incorporates many contingent features that determine the reference. For example, the reference of the name 'Ram' is determined, the causal theory says, by the historical conditions that are associated with the name-giving ceremony.[9] This is to say that, without there being any historical background to the naming ceremony, we could not have determined the referent of the name "Ram". Thus sense is not the determining factor; it is the contingent historical factors that make what a name refers to.

From the causal point of view, the sense of a name or any other expression depends not on an *a priori* sense but on the contingent causal conditions which are given in sense-experience. That is to say, sense, in the Fregean sense, cannot be involved in reference as the latter is purely a matter of fixing the designating function of a word. This theory, however, does not solve the problem of how the referent is fixed in the absence of a determinate conception of the object to be referred to. The objectual reference becomes a matter of pure chance since there is nothing in language that can tell what the word exactly refers to. Frege realized the gravity of the problem when he said that sense alone can determine reference and that sense is a logical rather than a causal entity. The idea is that sense is type-different from a cause which is a contingent entity. Causes can be empirically given but not the senses of the words. In fact it is a gross simplification of the situation if the sense is itself reduced to a causal event.[10] The non-Fregean approach to sense as a set of conventions also does not solve the problem since conventions themselves need sense if they are to be useful in fixing the reference.

There are two ways to approach the problem in the present context. They are (1) the largely Fregean way which consists in the primordiality of sense and (2) the grammatical way introduced by Wittgenstein. The Fregean way makes room for a purely *a priori* conception of sense such that through a logical method we capture the world in the network of language. The strategy of this method lies in the following steps:

First, the sentence of a language has compositional

normalcy: it has a well-formed sense.

Second, the sentence either asserts or denies the situation in the world: it is either true or false.

Lastly, a true or false assertion tells what and how the world is.

Thus from the way the sentence-formation takes place the sense is articulated in the sentence and further the sentence is declared true or false depending on what it tells about the world. Thus the world is necessarily known in the very process of our making a language-use. In the above strategy, the world is introduced as soon as the assertions take place. A mere sentence does not tell what the world is unless it is either asserted or denied. Frege thus made a tripartite division between sense, judgment or grasp of sense and the assertion of sense in the world.[11] While sense in itself is logically stationed in the logico-ontological realm, the grasp of sense is merely psychological and the assertion linguistic in character. The latter is the level of language intervening to make the judgement true or false. Here alone language and the world make contact. Thus Frege is aware that though sense itself is not involved in the world it comes into the world-order by being expressed in language. Language is the vehicle of truth and sense and there is the internal movement towards the world. In this way the Fregean route to the world is paved by sense within language.

The other route to the reality is charted by Wittgenstein in a grammatical way. This approach takes language as primordial in the sense that, for it, sense does not pre-exist language. Rather sense is located in language in that in language alone one ever asks what the sense of an expression is. Besides, for Wittgenstein, if sense would have been pre-linguistic, it would never have been internal to language and logic since the latter express only what is necessary and internal. Wittgenstein sees that the expression of sense demands the primordiality of language and its logic or grammar. In this sense it is the grammar that determines what sense the sentence has and what states of affairs it represents. That is, grammar determines what logical order the world has. This is accomplished through the determination of the sentence-order, its sense and truth-conditions. All these three components are accomplished in a fell swoop as all of them belong to the logical structure of the sentence. For Wittgenstein to be a sentence is to be a sentence with sense and truth-conditions. That is why sentence-sense is taken care of by the well-formed sentence itself.[12]

The grammatical way of Wittgenstein's fares better than Frege's since, in the latter, sense is divorced from language and made contingent to it. Thus there is no guarantee that sense can, in a determinate way, be expressed in language. In that case we have to regiment the language itself and reform it to make it the perfect medium of sense. This leads to many difficulties one being that sense has nothing to contribute to the word-order. That situation is remedied by making sense internal to language and also to the world-order. Grammatical nature of sense does stand as a defence against its being reduced to a causal event in the world. The referents of the words are guaranteed as the words are grammatically so designed that they cannot forfeit the referents if they remain meaningful in language. Thus grammar guarantees transparency so far as the world is concerned. It is only in grammar that we have the perfect representation of the world-order.

Now the question arises: what is it that sense does with regard to the world-order? and in what way does it do what it does? The most plausible answer is that sense makes the world intelligible. That is, sense 'presents' the world in the logical way so far as our conception of the world is concerned. Therein lies the logical order of the world which is the content of the conception of the world. The content can be like this: the world consists of the objects and their properties and relations. This content is the easiest to conceive as here we have a representation of the same in our thought and language. Language and thought are so structured that the contents of the world-picture and that of language are the same.

Here the notion of world-essence can arise which has a remarkably resilient structure in logic and metaphysics. The concept of essence comes closer to the notion of world-order as it is only in this notion that we can see the importance of sense. Sense itself is an essence and therefore is logical out and out. Sense reflects the structure of the sentence and therewith the structure of the world. Thus sense is not the constituent of a sentence but is, in fact, the essence of it. In that sense, by taking sense as the essence of language, we can discover the essence of the world. As Wittgenstein has said, essence is expressed in grammar[13] and has to be located only in grammar. Thus grammar and sense meet in their being concerned with the logical order of the world.

There is a view that the world-order is a matter of construction rather than of grammatical discovery. This is the view of those who think that sense is primarily a thought-content and is therefore mental. For them, sense is an instrument of construction and so must be taken as a matter of linguistic policy rather than as a grammatical fact. This leads to the view that the world-order is of our making[14] and thus has to be projected as a picture of our own. This anti-realist theory of sense gives up the Fregean pretensions of realism and makes a definite move towards the idea that sense is a matter of how we construe language and not how we take language as revealing. If we take it as reflecting the world-structure, then, in that sense, we have no escape from the idea that the world-structure is already given.

But this view forgets the Fregean dictum that without sense we cannot even determine what we can construct at all. The constructions themselves need a semantic space and so there is language already presupposed in all our activities. The world-picture presented by the language is precisely the one we need determine through sense. If the world is a construction, then it is all the more necessary that sense must be situated in the very structure of it. The world, in any case, is the one which is determined by sense. If anybody has a non-linguistic access to the world then only he or she can tell what it is for a world to be without sense. But such an access is impossible. The world is presented in language and language alone.

The grammatical strategy discussed so far makes room for the fact that truth and reference are both possible in the framewok of sense. Sense rules out the possibility of reference-failure in that it determines reference in a logical fashion. The causal determination of reference is overruled by the fact that reference is internally determined. The so-called vacuous names arise precisely because we have a determinate theory of reference in semantics. Besides, the truth-conditions themselves are logically determined as being ingrained in the structure of the sentence. Truth and reference thus having been internalized, the threat of semantic contingency and the resultant scepticism are ruled out. The possibility of the world being screened off from our semantic network is out of question because grammar stands as a logical guarantee against this possibility.

To sum up: the grammatical strategy secures a new way of fixing truth and reference. It lifts the ambiguity shrouding linguistic activity itself and also the mystery over the world-order. Thus language and the world are brought face to face in the structure of grammar.

Scrutability of Reference

Reference is the primary function of words and so necessarily language is linked with the world. This is evidenced in the fact that language has an in-built mechanism to refer to the world such that, in the very use of language, there is a talk of the world present. This basic fact has, however, been questioned by the semanticists like Quine and, to some extent by Davidson, in recent times. Their contention is that language does not necessarily make its reference to the world transparent and scrutable. The reason is that reference-links between the words and the objects are so variable that it is difficult to assign definite objects as referents of the words. The Fregean notion of unique reference is thereby replaced by the idea of variability and the inscruatability of reference.

There are two arguments leading to the thesis of inscrutability of reference. The first argument, as given by Quine,[15] is that, like meaning, reference is system-relative and so no reference can be fixed independently of the language-system in which the word occurs. This leads to the possibility that what is referred to in one system may not be the referent in another system thus making room for the fact that the word remaining the same the referent may change from system to system. This ushers in the indeterminacy in the reference of a word. Quine is arguing that the words have referents in the network of the conceptual system, and when the system itself changes, the words may acquire new meaning and reference. The second argument adduced by Davidson[16] is that reference is not a necessary condition of the truth-theory for a language, since language can manage to have the truth-laws and the links with the world without a theory of reference. That is to say, the reference can be dispensed with in stating the truth-conditions of the sentences.

Quine's inscrutability thesis arises because of the theory of ontological relativity he espouses. This is part of the naturalistic semantics that Quine upholds in deference to the holistic character of language and meaning. This naturalistic framework necessarily leads to the view that, if the conceptual scheme is holistic, everything, including ontology, must become relative to the system. Therefore there is no way we can talk of reference in the absolute sense. That implies that the ordinary conception of reference must be wrong as it tries to fix reference for a word independently of the language and the conceptual scheme. But, if we look into the working of the language as given in the natural setting, we can find that Quine's doubts about the determinacy of reference are misplaced because, in spite of the possibility of reference-change, there is a working stability in the referential mechanism of language. The words do show a remarkable stability in their grammatical behaviour such that we can, in all ordinary circumstances, tell what the referents of the words are. In exceptional cases, of course, we have to take the opinion of the experts as Putnam would like us to believe. The fact remains that system-dependency itself is not the cause of inscrutability of reference. Inscrutability can take place under a variety of circumstances which may not include the fact that words are dependent on the language we have. The very idea of alternative systems of interpretation of the reference of the words is a semantic myth as it leads to extreme scepticism regarding reference.

Davidson's argument for dropping reference altogether from a semantic theory does not conform to our intuitive understanding of language. For all practical purposes, the words refer and we are eager to use naming expressions in all sorts of ways. This goes towards establishing that a truth-theory may presuppose that a sentence is true or false on the condition that words constituting the sentence do refer. It is another matter that all words do not refer and that we are not always asked to spell out the reference of each word for the purpose of communication. It may so happen that a speaker can communicate without being aware that he or she has a definite reference for the words. In a sense language takes care of the reference of its words. Davidson is right in maintaining that language as a whole is responsible for the truth-conditions of the sentences and there is no piecemeal approach to the fixing of the references. But semantic holism cannot rule out the fact that words have not only meaning but also reference. There is no doubt an inner adjustment of the semantic theory of truth and that of reference.

The theory of ontological relativity is the background theory for the inscrutability thesis. This has resulted in the idea that the ontological entities posited in a conceptual system are not absolutely real.[17] They are real only as the posits in a language and thus they are part of the framework in which we think and live. Thus there follows what is called the relativization of the objects to the conceptual system. This necessitates the fact that words refer to these objects only as they are demanded by the system. But, as we can see, there is no *prima facie* reason for holding such a relativistic thesis in view of the fact that objects we talk about are not our posits, rather they are there independently of us. There is a system of objects no doubt but they are not relative to a pre-existing system of language. Language is as natural as the world itself and so there is no way of telling what the world is without presupposing language. But this does not entail that we can go beyond language to tell that the objects are relative to the language. The relativist thesis is, at best, a platitude and at worst inconsistent. Quine's imagery of Neurath's[18] ship being built while afloat does not solve the problem of how we can represent the remodelling of our conceptual scheme even while we do not have a vantage point outside the conceptual scheme. If the vantage point is available, there is no worry about relativism because we can always show that there is still a viewpoint which is not relative to anything.

The naturalistic semantics as such is subject to doubt because there is an inherent tendency to substitute the stimulus-response for the semantic facts of meaning and reference. This follows from Quine's abhorrence for the so-called intensional entities like meaning and reference. The words are nested in a linguistic network of behaviour and are therefore inextricably involved in the stimulus-response mechanism. Thus there is an interplay between the words and the stimulus-meaning they have. The latter is the prominent content of the linguistic use we make of the words and sentences. That shows that language becomes a part of the general behaviour of man and thereby it ceases to be an autonomous entity. This spells disaster for the semantics of reference and meaning.

The only way out of this semantic disaster is to restore reference and meaning to language and spell out the theory of meaning that makes room for truth and reference. This will be possible if naturalism is halted. Naturalism is by now the respected doctrine of those who believe that truth and reference are cognitive concepts for making language intelligible. They believe that language is a fact of nature and ought to be so taken. They further contend that meaning is not other than what we take words to mean in the natural setting. So there is scope for determining the setting in nature without creating meaning-entities. But this view grossly misrepresents the way meaning arises in language. Language is no doubt a natural phenomenon but that does not mean that the meaning itself is a causal and natural process. Meaning and reference are the way language functions *vis-a-vis* the world and are not themselves part of the fabric of the world. So there is a way of introducing meaning and reference via language and the language-user. Quine is therefore wrong in telling that meaning can disappear into the natural facts about language. Semantic scepticism is the worst disease that undercuts the very foundation of a theory of meaning and reference.

Reference is intact in a semantic theory since, without that, we cannot use a word in a sentence. The words are signs of the objects and their ideas. They do not copy the latter but they indicate their presence. From this point of view, words are as indispensable as the objects. In a representational system of language, the word-object relationship is pre-theoretically given and so there is no necessity of introducing reference-rules in the language except for the theoretical purposes. As we have already argued, the representationality of language depends much on the availability of reference. Both Frege and Wittgenstein argued for the indispensability of reference in the semantic system because they realized that, if truth is the basic concept, then there is bound to be reference to the world. The world-order must be pinned down in the language-system.

Holism, as laid down by Davidson, is not up against reference as such. Truth being central to the semantic structure, it is inevitable that the words themselves must refer to the world. Davidson wrongly argues that we can talk about the reality without reference[19] because to talk about the world is to refer to it. By referring, we are not creating a new world, rather we are making the existing world intelligible. The fear that a referring language interferes in the world is unfounded because in referring we are only instituting a way of reaching the world. How we do that depends upon the grammatical preparations we have already made, as Wittgenstein has told us. These preparations include a variety of postulation of meaning-rules and other semantic invariants like truth, necessity, etc. Holism is one such variety that tells us that grammatical rules always come as a whole and that there is nothing like making meaning a separable entity from truth, reference and the world.

Thus we can hope for a happy reunion of semantic holism and scrutability of reference. This can be achieved by systematizing semantics in the holistic way without sacrificing reference. The Representation Theory that we have espoused aims at making the linguistic representations holistic and at the same time makes a theory of meaning responsive to the demands of truth and reference.

Balancing Holism

The answer to Davidson's poser to reference is not the rejection of holism but the balancing of it against the demands of the truth-based semantics. Davidson is of the view that holism serves best the interest of truth and language within an empiricist framework. The immediate need of semantic holism is felt in accommodating truth in a linguistic framework that does not always make divisions between sentences and words, and also between what the sentences mean and what the words refer to. Davidson takes truth to the door of ordinary (natural) language all within the sweep of an axiomatic truth theory. The result is: a sweeping change in the very concept of truth. Truth no more requires a metaphysical grounding, it is self-sufficient in its operation in language. But this self-sufficiency does not free truth from language; rather the whole language is involved in the operation of truth. Thus holism is inevitable if truth is to be seen in the overall context of language.

Now let us see if holism is itself the answer to the demands of naturalistic semantics. Naturalistic semantics, as understood by Quine for instance, rejects the *a priori* idea of semantic necessity and opts for the standpoint that situates the semantic concepts in the natural history of language. This leads to the placement of truth in the behaviour-pattern of the linguistic community. This opens up, in the sequel, a steady invasion of naturalism into the domain of logic. Holism takes side with naturalism for the reason that a natural discourse is a total scheme of ideas and concepts all meshed up with human life. Thus holism is not a sequence of naturalism but is the methodological ally of it.

Even then holism, as against atomism, has both advantages and disadvantages. Its advantages are that it helps unify the discourse under the concept of truth and that it makes truth a prominent concept in that truth alone can provide the basis for a single theory of meaning for the whole language. But the disadvantages are that it dispenses with reference in a bid to make language autonomous and that it makes truth more and more an anthropological concept in view of the new-found love for the cross-cultural understanding and interpretation. Especially Davidson's Principle of Charity keeps truth tied to the cross-cultural phenomena in such a way that truth is a matter of how rational human beings understand the world. The Principle of Charity helps mobilize support for the community commitment to truth rather than error, but a community cannot always withstand the possibility of massive delusion. The mutual trust and reciprocity make a good deal of show of solidarity in the community but that does not rule out the possibility of error. This possibility may not be the direct result of holism but holism, in the global sense, does presuppose that human solidarity is the foundation of all our rational enterprise.

The possibility of making truth more and more human is open in the holistic framework. This may further erode the authority of truth if sufficient care is not taken to keep truth within the bounds of language. That means the classical notion of truth cannot be altogether dispensed with. The human face of truth must be in conformity with the conservative character of truth. This is realized by Davidson more than anyone else. According to him, even if truth is involved in the speaker-time network, there is an unchanging nature of truth that is impervious to the changing context. This shows that truth is basically a logical concept. Language changes and so do the contexts but truth does not change so far as its logical nature is concerned.

Thus holism has to be balanced with the demands for the security and stability of truth. Holism must allow for the possibility of independent characterization of truth. That will require a transparent semantics that ensures scrutability of reference. The new demand is that truth must reconcile to reference and other meaning-generating features as force and conventions. This requirement is part of the semantic strategy accepted in the representational theory of meaning.

Holism as such cannot lead us very far. It can at best show that truth is integrated into the linguistic and conceptual structure.

Besides, it shows that there is nothing like an atomization of truth since truth is a global concept. Many metaphysicians, like Hegel, had recognized this fact about truth but they failed to locate truth in language and had no conception of a semantic sense of the concept of truth. This drawback is removed by the semanticists who now make truth the basic concept in language. Semantic holism thus brings out the hidden meaning of linguistic representations in an integrated system of truths.

What characterizes truth theory in semantic holism is the fact of language-use in an integrated fashion. Here language is the background of all truth-talk. Language is the base of all truth-claims about the world. In the absence of the conception of language as a unique whole, even the truth-talk becomes less relevant. So it is realized that truth must be embedded in language since it is here that truth reveals what the world is. If truth were a non-linguistic concept, how could it tell what the world is? Telling what the world is requires language and that is precisely the argument that the limit of all truth-talk is language itself. Hence it must be owned that an integrated view of truth is always the best way of going about it.

Truth has a metaphysical dimension that leads Davidson to propound the theory of truth that closely follows an idealistic metaphysics.[20] Though it is not idealism as such, it could say that truth and reality are language-dependent in a very wider sense. That is, it could say that a holistic metaphysics is in order even if that metaphysics does not tell how the world is fully manifest in language itself. Semantic holism is silent over what makes the world so uniquely related to language but it tells also that truth alone can disclose this relationship. Thus truth becomes the only way to the unfolding of the nature of language and the world.

Truth and Being

The question of truth raises the question of being as it is in truth that the structure of being is unfolded. This is an unsolved problem in metaphysics that the nature of being is underlying our language and logic and that we presuppose rather than prove that the being is the bedrock of our scientific as well as non-scientific discourse. It is true that the question of being has not been properly raised in our contemporary semantics and metaphysics. From Frege to Davidson there is no clear-cut formulation of the problem of being. There is an effort in Wittgenstein to raise the question especially in his *Tractatus* but the question is largely brushed aside as a metaphysical issue.

Logic in the modern times has been so constructed that it has highlighted the world or reality only in a very fragmentary sense. In logic, the world of facts, rather than the world as such, is the reality that matters for the truth-value of the sentences. Frege, for instance, argued for the fact that the world consists of objects and concepts such that the sentences in language are true or false in relation to this world. This conception of the world, which is true for the linguistic philosophy in general, is in a sense very narrow as it does not raise the question of being. It only talks of the beings rather than being in the ontological sense.[21] This idea of being is as ancient as Plato and it is a tragedy that the basic concept is generally brushed aside, as Heidegger[22] has shown. The concept of being, being the primordial concept, is apt to be forgotten in our overwhelming concern for language and its semantic structure. It is therefore imperative that we bring in the concept to solve the outstanding problems in semantics and metaphysics.

Wittgenstein's *Tractatus* provides a turning point in the contemporary concept of being. Though Wittgenstein's problem here is largely logical and semantic, his interest lies in giving a new approach to the problem of being. Being is deliberately identified with what can be said, that is, the world of facts. The latter is what can be taken as represented in language. Such a view of being, of course, has its limits since it has led to a very positivistic notion of being. There is the obvious opposition to this view as it makes no distinction between the reality as it is given and the world as it is in itself. Realizing this Wittgenstein has provided a higher notion of being according to which the being-in-itself is that which cannot be said. It is the being that reveals itself in language and is therefore the ultimate form of all existence.

In a tone reminiscent of Heidegger's, Wittgenstein says that the higher reality is the bedrock being that is shown rather than said and must remain outside the purview of fact-stating language.[23] This notion of being has the Heideggerian character as it is said to be disclosed in language and yet it cannot be said in the factual sense. Being has a double character as it is both concealed and yet unconcealed in language. Here Wittgenstein adds that language is the primordial reality that discloses the being as without language we would not have encountered being at all.[24] The *Tractatus*, however, has failed to realize the full implications of the concept of being as it has made language an extensional system of representations. It has therefore failed in the effort to completely disclose the nature of being. Besides, it has not taken truth as a disclosure concept and so failed to tell how truth is the correlate of being.

Truth in extensional logic is more or less a representational concept and so there is a scope for truth to disclose the being at least partially. It is said that a sentence is true if only if the world is as it is depicted to be. This disclosure is important for under-standing the reality. But truth can disclose reality without being a direct correspondence between language and reality. Wittgenstein's notion of truth is bogged down in the picture conception of language and so does not transcend extensionalism. Heidegger openly revolts against this conception when he says that extensionalist metaphysics conceals the being rather than discloses it. Hence this metaphysics has to be overcome and there must be a fundamental ontology to bring the being back in the fold of human life. The *Dasein* is the true representative of the Being and philosophy must turn towards the concrete human world.[25]

Wittgenstein comes round this view in his later philosophy where he feels that being is the human forms of life and that being and truth are both disclosed in language. Language is the primordial reality that houses both being and truth. The language-games and the forms of life together constitute the disclosure of truth and being as, in language alone, there is the presence of being.[26] Being becomes the vital link between language and truth. Truth belongs to language and, at the same time, it is the other side of being so far as truth bears the marks of being. There is no non-grammatical way of grasping truth and being as grammar alone reveals the essence of truth and being.[27] The nature of being is still shown in language and thus there is the declared opposition to the metaphysical attempt to say what the being is.

The metaphysical discourse of being has always failed to understand being as it has tried to say the unsayable, according to Wittgenstein. The unsayable is the being that is the basis even of what we say, that is, of the world and so there cannot be an extra-linguistic way to reach the being. This makes Wittgentein bring the being into the open world of the human beings. Here the world is shareable and is in the human space of multiple forms of life. So being is recognizable as the totality of beings. Language speaks of itself and of the being that lies therein.

Semantics and metaphysics are both impossible if they try to say the unsayable. That is why the formal semantics of Frege and Tarski has to go if they fall into the metaphysical trap. This comes as a relief to those who advocate that truth theory is not a justification of language and that it is only a method of disclosing reality in language. Davidson has articulated it in so many words when he presents truth as an autonomous concept. Truth is the hallmark of language as without it we cannot have the notion of language at all. Language and truth are internally related such that truth indicates what language does in relation to the world.

If being is taken as the sum-total of all forms of life and language, we have a better access to the truth as truth itself is the sum-total all authentic language-games. Language-games reveal the structure of all existence including the being-in-the world and so truth is manifest in them. Truth cannot be something other than the being revealed in the language-games. So there is no way we can go about the truth except as it tells what the being is. Semantics in this sense does not disappear as in the semantic consciousness itself we are constantly reminded of being. Truth is the epitome of the semantic consciousness and so there is a direct link between the truth in language and the being of language and the world.

Thus it can be claimed that truth as a semantic notion does play a role in making it clear that language in the global sense is the home of being, to use the Heideggerian language. That is, there is reason to believe that truth discloses being, it being the seminal concept of our nearness to the being.

Being as World-Order

One may claim that the fundamental concept for logic and semantics is not being but the world-order. This may follow from the view that truth in the ordinary sense is concerned with the world as is given in sense-experience. The latter view is the one accepted by the majority of contemporary semanticists. So it is claimed that truth is either correspondence or coherence and not a disclosure as claimed by the Heideggerians. The latter view is the one that suits the framework of those who take being as primary. But being and the world-order are not the same and so truth in relation to them cannot be the same.

However, we can argue that being and the world-order are the same and that what is true of one is also true of the other. That is to say, what we mean by being is the same as what we mean by the world-order. This needs a non-Heideggerian approach to the concept of being. This approach is already available in the semantic and logical tradition with which we are concerned here. The concept of world-order is the basic concept in this tradition which is equivalent to the concept of being in metaphysics. Our concern is with the concept of word-order which is closely associated with the concept of logical form, on the one hand, and the concept of being, on the other.

The concept of logical form is the foundational concept in semantics since the latter is concerned with the world of meaning and thus tries to transcend the world of facts. Though extensional semantics takes the world of facts as inescapable, yet it sees, underlying the facts, the logical form of facts. Thus logical form is the underlying concept that gives semantics its logical character. The world of facts is the becoming which presupposes the being, the latter being the logical basis of the former. Thus the age-old distinction of being and becoming is given a semantic twist in the contemporary logical tradition. As we have already seen, the concept of truth is very much the semantic instrument through which the notion of being is introduced, as truth stands for the being in the logico-metaphysical scheme of things.

The effort of semantics is to transcend the world of becoming as in the latter lies the possibility of there being a breakdown of meaning and reference. Meaning may not hold its ground without it being rooted in the logical structure of language. Thus there is the necessity of introducing logical form as the basis of meaning. Therewith the notion of truth is introduced as the semantic feature of the logically well-formed sentences.

The first step towards establishing the semantic concept of being and logical form is to recognize the concept of what the traditional metaphysicians called the Form or the Substance. The notion of Form[28] in Plato has indicated that there is a permanent basis of language and experience and that that permanent principle alone can meet the demands of transcendence from the tyranny of facts. Thus in the Western tradition there arose the metaphysics of the permanence underlying epistemology and logic. With Hegel the notion of Form got transformed into the notion of Reason[29] as the metaphysical ground of knowledge and experience. The need now was felt to give an idealistic bent to the inquiry of being and form. The being-becoming dichotomy was resolved in the synthesis of the reason and experience in a dialectical framework. Hegel's experiments, however, have not gone waste in the contemporary logical tradition. We have inherited the legacy of being in the logical notion of form as indicated in the works of Frege and Wittgenstein. Thus modern semantics still echoes the Plato-Hegelian appeal to the permanent principle of being and form.

The most important step taken by semantics is the one of identifying the being with the logical form of the world or the world-order. This became inevitable since language analysis required the notion of the world-order not only for explaining meaning but also truth. Philosophy of language presupposes that there is a world and that there is something rather than nothing. This metaphysical presupposition indicates that, that something which exists is not a mere factual and contingent world, but that it is the being or the reality as such. The latter is the essence of all worlds we can conceive of. That is the form of the world. Wittgenstein's *Tractatus* has given a very graphic representation of the concept of the form of the world.[30] The notion of the form of the world is the unique notion of how the world is to be conceived as such and that entails that there is the world-essence that can be represented in logic. The world-essence constitutes the ultimate structure of the world that is the foundation of meaning and truth in language. This is also called the world-order that is the subject-matter of logic to explain. It is in this sense that semantics brought in the concept of logical form of the world as the equivalent of the metaphysical concept of being.

Let us see how the concept of world-order is the foundation of modern semantics. First of all, it is the notion of the world which is the basis of all language and so language itself stands as the surety of the world. There is no other guarantee of the world than the fact that we speak and use language which represents the world. Second, though language represents the world in its totality, what we are interested in is the structure of language and its relation to the structure of the world. The latter is our main concern since the world-order is the typical concern of the metaphysician interested in knowing the foundations of language. Thus we are led to postulate that the world-order is the foundation of language. Lastly, the world-order is the being as such that is the essence of all existence and is the metaphysical reality that lies at the basis of our inquiry into meaning and truth.

Now the question arises, why is it that a semantic perspective should be concerned with the being or the world-order? The answer lies in the fact that semantics gives an image of this world-order in its conceptual network. The meaning-relations and the truth-laws all presuppose that the sentences are concerning the world and that in them the form of the world is already reflected. This brings in the idea that there is a projection-relation between language and the world. This idea is highlighted in the semantics of truth, though not in the explicit form as in Wittgenstein's *Tractatus*. The semanticists concerned with truth admit that truth-laws are the laws of linguistic projections. This becomes the mainstay of the truth-based semantics in that these projections are all logical in character.

The linguistic projections are such that they indicate that there is a parallel between the form of language and the form of the world or the world-order. This parallelism is of the following kind:

LOGOS → BEING

REASON → WORLD-ORDER

LANGUAGE → WORLD

For logos there is the corresponding being, for reason the world-order and for language there is the world. This is the parallelism between what is conceived to be language and logic, on the one hand, and what is taken as real, on the other. Here is what semantics presents as the interface between the being or the form of the logical kind and the form of the reality. This ensures that language represents the world-order in its own essence and makes truth and meaning possible.

The centrality of the notion of form to language and the world is unique to philosophy of language in general. Cassirer in his *Philosophy of Symbolic Forms*[31] has said that language being the basis of all inquiry into the reality it is imperative that meaning is the ground of all existence. That is, the symbolic forms are the basic constituents of all reality in the sense that there is nothing real that is not grounded in the symbolic forms. This general principle is fully articulated in the semantic tradition where the logical form of language and that of the world become identical. This is as much found in Frege as in Wittgenstein. Davidson has articulated it in the idea that there is nothing we can think of that is not already involved in language.

The metaphysical concept of the logical structure of the world is the mainstay of the semantic inquiry since on this idea our very idea of truth and meaning depends. Meaning is the articulation of the expressive character of language and this requires the idea of the world being logically well-ordered. Only a logiclly well-ordered world can ensure stable meaning. The world must be so constituted that it can offer linguistic rules that can capture that regularity. Thus grammar of language requires a stable world. That stability, however, is not a contingent feature of the world. It is, in fact, the necessary feature of the world. Thus semantics is the study of this necessary structure of the world. The concept of truth indicates this logical structure in a more pronounced way. Truth is the feature of the sentences that represent the world. This representation would not have been possible if the world would not have a logical structure. Thus there is a convergence of all semantic concepts in the notion of the logical form or the being of the world. The symbolic structure of language bears testimony to the fact that the world is well-ordered and there is a rational structure of reality.

Symbolic Forms and the Representations of the World

The idea of symbolic forms already introduced makes a move towards establishing the fact that language is the central concern of the philosophy of the world-order. Language is the totality of the activities that relate to the world and in this lies the revelation of the world and its rational order. Without language this order would ever remain undisclosed. We can therefore call this world-order the logo-centric order that demands that language and its conceptual structure be central to the conception of the world.

The symbolic forms are diverse and multifaceted. As Cassirer has pointed out, there are all types of symbolic forms such as myth, science, art and religion[32] and in all there is the symbolic activity of articulating the projected reality. In all these forms of symbolic activity, there is the definite way of reaching the reality and manifesting it in language. We can say that, in all these symbolic activities, language is the primary reality and that in language alone these forms of activity are organized. From this we can further conclude that language and meaning constitute the basis of all kinds of symbolic representation.

There is a basic continuity between symbolic forms and the representations of the reality. All symbolic forms are representations of the reality that constitutes the subject-matter of those forms. The mythic reality is not far removed from the scientific reality and the latter from the religious. Thus there is a continuity throughout the realm of representations. The representations are the articulations of the world-order and therefore the world-order in mythology is not different from that of science. Yet there is a difference which lies in the organization of the world-order itself. Science organizes it differently from that of mythology. Both represent two world-views.

Now the question is: in what way is representation in language the key to the reality? This is the basic issue for us so far as we are concerned with the notion of truth and world-order. As already indicated, language is the source of all symbolic forms and so is the basis of all thought about the world. It is therefore necessary that we understand the nature of thought and language in order to understand the world itself. Herein lies the idea that we can no longer understand the world in the human consciousness itself. This was the belief earlier that the world is revealed in human consciousness. Hegel idealistically concluded that the world is the mind objectified. This theory presupposes an independent reality called the mind or consciousness. This standpoint has its limitations as it abolished the role of language altogether. Language is a mere shadow of the consciousness from this standpoint. But the philosophy of symbolic forms transforms this idea into the one of making language prior to even consciousness, and thus the world is no more revealed in consciousness except in language itself.

From our standpoint, the world is not a projection of the mind as mind itself needs something more basic for its own intelligibility. Language gives meaning to mind as in the former alone the mental representations of reality are articulated and made intelligible. Thus language becomes the basic phenomenon for understanding thought and reality. The so-called mental contents[33] which are taken as the repository of meaning and structure are intelligible only in language. This obliges us to make mind and its represen- tations dependent on the language in which they are embedded. This has the additional implication that meaning is independent of the mental contents and representations. There are two issues here which need probing. They are (1) the representationality of the mental contents and (2) the mental contents as ontological entities. The mental contents are representational only insofar as the language in which they occur is representational and secondly, the mental contents are ontologically derivative. That is, they are not substantial entities which can be taken as representing the world. Only linguistic symbols are representational. Mental contents as involved in symbols do represent the world. In this we can say that the content theory of representations is superseded by the symbolic theory of representations.

It has been said that mental structures determine the world-order. C.I. Lewis in his *Mind and the World Order*[34] has held that the functions of the mind pragmatically determine the structure of the world. According to him, the categories of the mind together constitute the scheme that makes the world as it is. This theory makes it clear that mind is the basis of the world-order. But this theory does not take into account the fact that even these mental structures have a linguistic reality and that they need a linguistic medium for their articulation. So the world-order is not mental but linguistic in essence. Language is an autonomous reality and its representational character is original to it. Mind and its categories are all language-dependent.

Meaning, which is the basic feature of language, is not derived from anything other than language itself. Mind is not the store-house of meaning as it is the meaning which is basic to the concept of representation as such. Representations, whether mental or linguistic, presuppose meaning. So there cannot be any realm, mental included, which is prior to semantics and its structures. Thus what needs an autonomous existence is the language and its meaning. Truth follows as a matter of meaning going representational.

To conclude: truth is the index of the fact that language represents the world and also that language is the harbinger of meaning into the world-order. The world-order is the basic desideratum of all speech and other language-games. The symbolic forms represent the world-order in all its logicality and rationality.

References

1. *See* Wittgenstein, *Tractatus Logico-Philosophicus*, tr. by D.F. Pears and B.F. McGuinness (Routledge and Kegan Paul, London, 1961). (To be abbreviated as *Tractatus* hereafter).

2. For a discussion on this idea *see* J.L. Mehta, *The Philosophy of Martin Heidegger* (Banaras Hindu University, Varanasi, 1967), Chapter 10. *See also* George Steiner, *Heidegger* (Fontana Press, London, 1978).

3. Frege, *The Foundations of Arithmetic*, tr. by J.L. Austin (Blackwell, Oxford, 1950).

4. *See* Russell, *Introduction to Mathematical Philosophy* (Allen and Unwin, London, 1919) Chapter XIV.

5. *See* P.F. Strawson, "On Referring", in *Classics of Analytic Philosophy*, ed. by R. Ammerman (Tata McGraw-Hill Publishing Company, Bombay-New Delhi, 1965).

6. *Tractatus* 3.2-3.23.

7. For a discussion on sentence-holism, *see*, Bhartṛhari, *Vākyapadiyam* I tr. by Satyakam Verma (Munshiram Monoharlal, New Delhi, 1970).

8. *See* Saul Kripke, "Naming and Necessity", in *Semantics of Natural Language*, ed. by Davidson and Harman (D. Reidel, Dordrecht, Holland, 1972). For further discussion, *see* Devitt and Sterelny, *Language and Reality* (Blakwell, Oxford, 1987) Chapter 5.

9. *Ibid.*

10. *See* Christopher Peacocke, "Content and Norms in a Natural World", in *Information, Semantics and Epistemology* ed. by E. Villaneuva (Blackwell, Oxford, 1990).

11. Frege, "Thoughts", in *Logical Investigations*, tr. by P.T. Geach (Blackwell, Oxford, 1977).

12. *Tractatus*, 5.473.

13. Wittgenstein, *Philosophical Invesatigations*, tr. by Anscome (Blackwell,Oxford,1953) sect.373. (To be abbreviated as *PI* hereafter).

14. C. Wright, *Wittgenstein on the Foundations of Mathematics* (Duckworth, London, 1980).

15. *See* Quine, "Things and Their Place in Theories", in *Theories and Things* (Harvard University Press,Camb. Mass.,1981).

16. *See* Davidson, "Reality Without Reference", in *Inquiries into Truth and Interpretation* (Blackwell, Oxford, 1984).

17. Quine,"Ontological Relativity", in *Ontological Relativity and Other Essays* (Columbia University Press, New York,1969).

18. *Ibid.*

19. Cf. Davidson,"Reality Without Reference", pp. 215-25.

20. Cf. "The Method of Truth in Metaphysics", in *Inuiries into Truth and Interpretation*, pp.199-214.

21. *See* Heidegger, *Being and Time*, tr. by John Macquarrie and Edward Robinson (Basil Blackwell, Oxford,1962).

22. *Ibid.*

23. *Tractatus*, 6.522.

24. Speech is the essence of Being for both Wittgenstein and Heidegger. For both Being is shown in language.

25. Cf. Heidegger, *Being and Time*, Introduction.

26. *PI* sect. 50.

27. *Ibid.*, sect. 371-373.

28. *See* Plato, *The Republic*, tr. by Benjamin Jowett (Airmont Publishing Company, Inc., New York, 1968).

29. *See* Hegel, *The Phenomenology of Mind*, tr. by J.B.Baillie (Allen and Unwin, London,1910).

30. *Tractatus*, 4.12-4.121.

31. E. Cassirer, *The Philosophy of Symbolic Forms* vol. I, tr. by R. Manheim (Yale University Press, New Haven,1955).

32. *Ibid.*

33. Cf. J. Fodor, *Psychosemantics* (MIT Press,Camb. Mass,1988).

34.   C.I. Lewis, *Mind and the World-Order* (Dover Publications, Inc., New York, 1929).

5

The Ways of Meaning : Realism and Anti-Realism

In this chapter I will deal with the problem of meaning in the context of the recent debate between realism and anti-realism about meaning. The debate is of recent origin so far as semantics is concerned. It is about whether meaning is a matter of truth-conditions of the sentences or it is concerned with the assertion-conditions of the sentences. The problem arises because meaning has been generally associated with truth of the sentences and truth itself is a very general concept that needs a realist framework for its understanding. So realism was inevitable for the understanding of truth as we have seen in the preceding chapter.

The question of whether truth is the basic concept in semantics was raised by the philosophers as it was found that meaning is not dependent on any other concept such as truth and that the semantic significance of meaning must remain confined to the framework of the use of language. The later Wittgenstein emphasized the fact that meaning is a matter of how language functions and not a matter of the sentences being true or false pictures or representations of the world. Thus there is, apparently, a tendency among the later Wittgensteinians to project a kind of anti-representationalism as the basis of the anti-realist theory of meaning.

The present chapter seeks to define the strict boundaries of the so-called realistic and anti-realistic theories of meaning and to show that the representationalism that we have espoused is not threatened by the anti-realist semantics. The contention is that representationalism does not impose either a realistic or non-realistic semantics on us. A holistic semantics is still available to make truth relevant to the meaning of the sentences without making the latter dependent on the former.

Truth and Meaning

Meaning is the semantic phenomenon that accrues to the sentences and their interrelated network in language. Language is the broad field of the linguistic actions that we naturally engage in. Thus there is a vast network of language-games that constitute the field of language.[1] This field is the totality of the linguistic activities that make a whole such that every possible language-use can be entertained within its scope. This presupposes the idea that language has a time-dimension in which all possible uses of language, past, present and future can be serialized, that is, can be put on a time-scale such that this makes language spread over infinite time and space. It is in this network that meaning arises as a basic phenomenon.

Two concepts emerge along with meaning: one, the idea of language being in constant proximity with the world, that is, language being involved in the world and second, the idea of language representing the world in the sense that it tells what the world is. Thus the idea of truth emerges on the scene with the force of a semantic necessity. Meaning thus learns to co-exist with truth and representation in language. Neither meaning nor representation is responsible for truth to arise nor is it the other way round. Truth does not make meaning arise in the way it is understood ordinarily. All the three, that is, truth, meaning and representation co-exist in close semantic harmony such that it is difficult to detach one from the other. Hence the question of explaining their relation.

Frege and Wittgenstein drew our attention to this semantic harmony of truth and meaning in language. Frege led to the idea that truth is a very important concept in semantics and logic, and yet it itself presupposes the meaning or sense of the sentences. Sense, according to him, is the very basis .of language and so everything that language does ultimately depends on sense. In this sense, for Frege, there is a unique ontological priority of sense over truth and the rest of the semantic concerns. Wittgenstein has not been concerned with the ontological priority of sense at all, though he also believes that sense is logically prior to truth in language. This is so because, according to him, truth matters to the sentences only when they are representations of the world. But meaning is the primordial structure of the sentences themselves. Thus there is semantic reason why truth must logically follow meaning rather than the other way round.

It has been generally believed that the classical semantics of Frege is wedded to the concept of truth and so there is, for him, only a truth-based semantics available. This impression has been created by the Fregeans who have taken the Frege of the *Grundlagen*[2] as the model of semantic analysis of language. But in this there is hardly any semantics except in the remote sense that the truth of mathematical sentences is considered. The idea of sense is absolutely lacking here so much so that the sense-reference distinction, which is so crucial to the Fregean semantics, is absent in this text. Frege of the "On Sense and Reference"[3] is most competent to open up the debate regarding the relation between truth and meaning or sense. For him, the truth of sentences is a matter of reference and not of sense. Only when the sentences refer to the world they have the property of truth and falsity. Sense accrues to the sentence even before there is a referential link with the world. Therefore sense is a unique semantic category that tells that a sentence is meaningful even when truth of the sentence is not at stake. How this happens is a matter of detailed analysis which we shall go into later.

The semantic primordiality of sense is a very important concept in philosophical semantics. This is reiterated by Wittgenstein. In the *Tractatus* he has shown[4] that sense is the essential structure of the sentences and that it is shown in the very structure of the latter. Wittgenstein's main problem was as to how we can account for the sense of the sentences without knowing how the sentences refer to the world, that is, how we can understand the meaning of the sentence without knowing how each sentence is linked with the world. The solution of the problem lies in telling that the sentence-sense is autonomous so far as the conditions under which we come to know it is concerned. These conditions are all grammatical in nature, and yet they do not constitute the sense but reveal it in the practice of language. Sense is independent of the reference of the sentence to the world because sense is itself the ground of this reference. Wittgenstein helps us realize that sense itself could not be made dependent on reference because there is no way to explain how a reference-dependent sense can be really semantically autonomous.

For both Frege and Wittgenstein, sense is the ideal content of language that is manifested or expressed in language. This content is neither a psychological content nor a physical entity such that there is no reason to fear that sense is lost for ever in the mental and physical world. It is the grammatical structure that expresses it and in a sense gives it the dignity it deserves. Wittgenstein is more explicit on the grammatical-logical structure of sense insofar as the basic linguistic expressibility of sense or meaning is concerned.

Now the main problem is, how are truth and sense related in

the perspective of representation? Representation is a fundamental concept according to which language is basically a representation of the world. Thus, in this context, it is imperative to note that there could be no relation between language and the world unless there is a logical link between the linguistic representations and the world. This link is facilitated by truth since a true representation is a true picture of the world. Truth has often been identified as a relation between a sentence or assertion and the world. This relation is a formal concept of taking language to the heart of the world. It is the business of semantics to identify the conditions under which this formal relation holds good. Frege held that sense provides these conditions as sense alone determines the conditions under which the sentence is true. Sense is neutral to both truth and falsity, and yet without it truth and falsity would not arise. Thus, in the Fregean framework, truth and world are mediated by sense or meaning. Sense brings language back to the world and in the process it shows that the symbiotic relation between language and the world must be deposited in sense itself.

The interface between language and the world is the handiwork of sense and truth. First of all, sense makes the interface rigid and nomological as it alone confers on the language-world relationship the bond of necessity. A language with sense is a language about the world. Sense makes the relation necessary and gives rise to the possibility of truth-values. Thus semantics is born out of the sense going the way of the language and the world. This idea is better clarified in Wittgenstein than in Frege as in the former it is clear that truth becomes the matter of the operational property of language because sense already has prepared the ground for it. Sense makes it objectively real that truth must accrue to a proposition if its intention is to represent the world. The question of representation is not contingent to language; it is its necessary structure.

Is truth accidental to the whole semantic discourse? This question has bothered the semanticists for the reason that, if truth is accidental, then there will be a threat to language as such since the latter may itself become accidental. Hence it has been admitted that truth is a necessary property of all assertions about the world. The logic of language says that truth is a necessary feature of all representational discourse such that there is no way of dismantling the logic of truth from the logic of language. Language and truth fall into the same logical space.

The guarantee of truth being essential to language is provided by the sense of language as sense or meaning is the autonomous pre-truth reality of language. This is so because sense determines truth and does not follow it. If sense follows truth, then sense will be contingent in itself as it is now a creature of the new constellation of truth, language and the world. But this possibility is ruled out since sense itself is pre-truth and so must precede the emergence of truth in language.

Davidson has a slightly different theory here as he maintains that sense or meaning and truth are co-terminus, that is, are interdependent rather than truth depending on meaning. His argument is that truth, being a necessary part of language, must be its inmost structure and so there is no meaning which does not partake of this structure. Thus, at one level at least, that is, at the depth-structure level, there is the sameness of meaning and the truth-conditions.[5] The truth-conditions are the inner conditions of meaning of the sentences. Davidson is aware that truth itself is not a derivable concept and so there is no other way of explaining it except by relating the sentence to the world by the Tarski-formula of Convention T. But that formula itself explains meaning as well if we can convert it into a Convention M. Thus Davidson is after a unification of the conditions of meaning and truth in his holistic framework.

The weakness of this framework is, however, revealed in the idea that truth and meaning are the same partners in the linguistic representations of the world. The weakness is that this sameness in partnership is due to an accidental constellation of the truth-conditions and the meaning-conditions. Language is fortunate enough to find that what are its truth-conditions are at the same time its meaning-conditions. It is not necessary that in all cases truth-conditions are available and secondly, even if they are available, they may not be the same as the meaning-conditions. Meaning is always presupposed by the truth-conditions as even the talk of truth-conditions must have meaning. How does Davidson explain that truth-conditions are available in a metalanguage? Is not the meaning of the metalanguage sentences themselves presupposed?

Our solution is that meaning is autonomous of truth and thus needs no explanation in terms of truth-conditions. But this does not imply that truth-conditions are not available at all. In fact, semantically speaking, truth-conditions are the immediate objects of semantic explanation as it has been claimed by the semanticists. The point is that, under certain conditions only, there is a coincidence of truth-conditions and meaning. This does not at all imply that Davidson's framework does not work at all. It rather works so well for certain parts of our language that it seems so certain to apply all over our discourse.

Truth and Meaning as Disclosures

As argued earlier, truth could be viewed as a disclosure of reality in the sense that it tells what the structure and the content of the world is. Truth is so world-bound that, once it is grasped, it reveals the structure of the world. For example, we take the sentence "Snow is white" and try to know its truth. We can find that its truth depends on what the actual world is. The world contains objects called snow which are white. Thus not only the contents but also the structure of the world are represented by truth. Thus knowing the truth means knowing the world as it is. In this sense, we can say that truth is the linguistic means of getting onto the world.

Meaning, on the other hand, is not so obviously a case of

disclosure. It makes disclosures about language rather than about the world. Anyway, meaning is a disclosure concept though in a different sense. Meaning tells what language is and what it is capable of doing. That is, it reveals the inner secrets of the language. For example, if the language is a fictional discourse, its meaning tells that it is concerning the fictional objects. Meaning of language is like a mirror because as soon we see it we can know what the language is and what it is about. As Davidson has rightly said,[6] in knowing the meaning, we know the beliefs and other intentional conditions of the sentences. That is, we know everything about the sentence, the beliefs it expresses and the thought it conveys. Thus a whole meaning-world is presented by the sentence. This could be construed as a disclosure such that meaning is articulate about language and perhaps indirectly about the world.

Frege himself has shown that sense is a disclosing device that makes language transparent in its structure and function. Sense is the thought that reveals itself and also the language in which this revelation takes place. Besides, sense also reveals the world which language represents. Thus the Fregean doctrine of sense is a doctrine of disclosure of the world and language so far as the world and language are logically linked. One may wonder how the Fregean sense can disclose anything other than itself in the absence of a disclosing medium. Since language itself requires sense for its own revelation it cannot itself be the disclosing medium. But Frege's underlying assumption is that language is not a mere disclosing medium; it is the only locus of sense itself. So sense not only discloses what the language itself is but also it thereby tells what the world is. Language is not a screen for sense, it is its disclosing function. That is, language is the very disclosing activity of sense. In this sense it is clear that sense is the activity of disclosure itself. The world's disclosure is the representational function of sense and language. The world could have been undisclosed but for language and sense. This is known as the idea that the world could be the reality as it is, even if language might not have come into existence. But once language is there there is no way of disclosing the world except through language.

Wittgenstein has added the view that meaning, in spite of its disclosing function, need not be an ideal entity in the sense it has been postulated by Frege that sense is such a timeless entity. The ideality of sense does not prohibit it from discharging its disclosing function, however. Meaning is as much real as the language of which it is the meaning. Meaning sheds its ideality in the process of becoming the disclosing entity. As meaning bears on the language and its representing function it becomes the real and objective entity. The shedding of ideality is not the disappearance as such from the scene of language as it has been claimed by the opponents of the reality of sense.[7] It is true that meaning is not a hidden structure but it does not mean that it is nothing, for that matter. The deconstructionist view of the matter is that the sense or meaning is not a metaphysical reality[8] and that it is something as fragile as the linguistic habits themselves. The language-games which are the only available forms of language demonstrate that meaning is not other than the linguistic nuances themselves. This view makes it obligatory to see meaning as the conventional product of our language-forms.

Our argument is that meaning as the disclosure of language and the world is as real as the language and the world. That is, if language and its representing functions are real, meaning cannot be less real even if it is the case that language is a stream of functions and uses. Meaning is not an item of the stream but nonetheless it is an item of language as such since, without it, the stream of language cannot be thought about at all. In this sense, meaning can be called a grammatical reality or the grammatical essence. By this, however, it is not meant that grammatical reality is a hidden structure or an ideal entity in the metaphysical sense. Yet it remains the reality as it is grasped by the speakers as well as the listeners. Thus there is no lack of transparency or perspicuity so far as the reality of meaning is concerned.

Thus there are three ways in which meaning-as-disclosure view can be pressed. First, it can be shown that meaning is for transparency and perspicuity. It is for making things and phenomena clear. Secondly, meaning is the representation of the world as the latter is disclosed in language. Thirdly, meaning is the method of understanding of language and the world. Thus there is meaning as the expression of the contents of language and the world. We will call this view the immanent view of meaning. This view represents meaning as the grammatical reality of language. The other way of undrestanding meaning is that meaning discloses itself into consciousness and thereby there is a manifestation of meaning in language. This view has its origin in the idealist tradition in Western metaphysics. Cassirer[9] in his theory of symbolic forms has pointed out that meaning is the underlying ideal structure of symbols and these structures are the ideal contents of the transcendental consciousness. Besides, it has been held that meaning of the language-structures is in the thought-structures of the language-users. Husserl claims that meanings are the ideal essences underlying the structure of consciousness, that is, they are the intentionalities[10] which constitute the very structures of consciousness. This view takes meaning as real in the logical sense and yet it holds that meaning cannot be removed from transcendental consciousness. There are many difficulties in this view. One such difficulty is that meaning is made a mental entity and thereby its semantic character is compromised. Besides, as a mental entity, meaning ceases to be a disclosure of language and the world. As a meaning in the consciousness, it is dependent on the latter, that is, on the consciousness for its own disclosure. Thus meaning ceases to be autonomous. This view of meaning can be called the externalist theory of meaning that tends to take meaning as a derivative concept.

Language, Fields and Meanings

Now the question is, how does one explain meaning if meaning is a matter of language and not of consciousness? If meaning is a matter of language then no explanation of meaning is possible since the language in which this explanation takes place needs meaning. Thus meaning becomes an ineffable phenomenon.[11] That is, meaning cannot itself be explained since we cannot explain it anywhere except in language. This view seems to be inevitable if we really want to explain meaning. Explanation causes this difficulty as it needs a language of explanation. But otherwise it raises no problem.

The externalist view more openly advertises for explanation of meaning and so it does say that meaning is not in the language itself but in the consciousness. But, if meaning is a matter of consciousness, then it can be asked how can we explain meaning except in the consciousness itself? Consciousness is itself in need of meaning and so there is no escape from circularity in explanation. If, however, meaning can be explained by consciousness there is reason to believe that there is nothing in meaning which is not in consciousness itself. That makes meaning and consciousness the same thing. This is the price of idealism one has to pay if one chooses to ignore the autonomy of meaning.

The view that meaning is a disclosure tells that there is a way out of this dilemma of making meaning ineffable or making it non-autonomous. Meaning is part of the field of language in which it discloses language and the world. The field is the field of language-games that make the play of meaning-disclosure possible. Thus there is the possibility of understanding language as a field of linguistic activities in which meanings are necessarily disclosed. This idea is already implicit in Wittgenstein's notion of a language-game. The suggestion is that a language-field bears the total burden of the meaning-disclosures.

Meaning brings, along with it, the idea of thought and

language as the representation of the world. The representations are given in the field of language. Language, as a field, contains the possibility of its own generation as a representing medium and also as a meaning-bearing mechanism. Thus both the ideas of expressing meaning and also constituting the world are present in the field of language. The question of the world being constituted arises because the world that is represented is the world that is meaningful in the language. Unless the world is thus reproduced in language, it cannot assume the meaningfulness bestowed by language. Thus both meaning and the world are integrated in language.

The field as such is an open system of concepts and categories all symbolically integrated in language. Here therefore are two ways of understanding the field. First, there is the idea that language consists of the linguistic symbols all bound up with the linguistic rules. Second, these symbols carry the schemes of categories that express the thought-structures expressed in the language. Thus thought and language become one seamless reality. Added to this is the fact that the field is a dynamic medium of activity. That is signified by the word 'force' which contains the idea that the symbols and the categories are dynamic processes of activity. Each is the functional field of other-regarding actions such as referring, describing and other linguistic activities. Innumerable are the ways the symbols can function. Each may be called a speech-act, as Austin[12] has pointed out. The speech-acts need not be narrowly viewed as the performances undertaken in language but as the scheme of doing linguistic acts in conformity with the total field of language. Austin lacks the idea of a total field of language and therefore fails to locate the specific speech-acts in the right context. The topography[13] of the speech-acts must be redrawn through the notion of field rather than speech-act itself.

The following is the way the field concept can help reorganize the concept of speech-act. The latter is not itself internally divided into the locutionary, illocutionary and perlocutionary[14] acts since these are only local divisions within the field of language. So the field absorbs all these internal divisions and sub-divisions in its total scheme of symbols. The field theory can cement these divisions in order to present a holistic view of language. Language itself always functions as a system and so the location of the units of speech-act is facilitated within the total scheme.

The idea of force is the continuing legacy that binds the field theory to the theory of speech-acts. This idea is the greatest contribution of Austin to theory of language. Force is that mechanism by which language is made into a system of activities. It introduces the dimension of relating the symbol to the intention of the speaker. As Grice and Strawson have admitted, the intention-dimension[15] of language cannot be neglected if language has to be seen as a system of activities. The intention underlying language-games provides the clue to the inner dynamics of the symbolic activities.

Meaning is the totality of force, intention and the sense accruing to the symbol system. The force is the index of what the symbol is used for, say, in describing, representing and in giving orders, etc. There is no force-neutral symbol-use as every symbol manifests a way of its being used in a certain context. Then the intention introduces the speaker's interest and his goals as he manifests them in the network of speaker-hearer communication. Meaning is not a product of the speaker-hearer intentionality, but takes care of these intentions in order to facilitate the communication between the speakers of the language. Lastly, the sense of the linguistic symbols can be better understood as the bedrock of the force and intention. Sense provides the semantic background for the emergence of force and intention. In this sense meaning is the basic concept even for force and intention.[16]

Now the question is, is there a connection between force and the field view of language? The field itself contains a force of its own which does not depend on an external source. The pragmatic notion of force has its origin in the idea that language has to be used externally by a speaking community and that force is legitimized as a community principle of manipulating the symbols. But this view has limitations of its own. First of all, it converts language into an instrument of communication and secondly, it makes meaning an accidental feature of language. Both these limitations can be removed by the field theory by tracing out the origin of force to the language as such. If language is a dynamic system of symbols then there is reason to believe that force is built into the language itself. So there is a necessary relation between language and force. Force is recognized as the very dynamics of language by both Frege and Wittgenstein. Whereas Frege called it the underlying dimension of making language relevant to the world, Wittgenstein made it the very source of the idea that language-games are the forms of life of the language-users. Force is thus taken as the internal source of the linguistic activities. Austin has, however, made it the external means of making a performative utterance possible. Besides, for him, meaning is a distinct phenomenon from force, though both are co-present in the speech-act itself.

In field theory of language there is a unification of both meaning and force. The apparent duality of meaning and force is dissolved for the sake of making meaning the very essence of force and *vice versa*. If force is a semantic concept, then there is no reason why meaning or sense cannot itself generate the force. For example, if a sentence is a command then its force of a command has its locus in the sentence-sense itself. It is not that the sense is pre-existing the force but rather that the force that arises is due the sense found in the sentence itself. The structure of a command is the index that it is meant as a particular linguistic act. So force must be ingrained in meaning itself.

Truth-Conditions and the Field of Language

In this context, the question arises, what role do the truth-conditions play in explaining meaning? This question is important since the semanticists are of the opinion that truth-conditions do matter in explaining meaning. Two things are important here: one, the idea of truth as a semantically basic concept and second, the idea of truth-conditions as the constitutive grounds of meaning. Both these ideas are of the semantic kind which any account of meaning is likely to encounter. In the logico-semantic tradition it is taken for granted that truth-conditions are a *sine qua non* of all meaning-relations amongst the propositions. It is argued by the semanticists like Carnap[17] and others that there are no sentential connections which are not truth-conditionally explained. That is, according to them, truth-conditions hold the key to the logical structure of the sentences. The *Tractatus* itself held the view that truth-conditions do present the logical face of the sense of the sentences so far as they are the pictures of the reality.[18] In this sense, it is undeniable that truth-conditions have been logically associated with the meaning of the sentences. In recent years it is Davidson who has propounded the view that truth-conditions alone suffice to account for meaning since, according to him, the truth-conditions and meaning are the same thing.[19]

The above view about meaning is generally identifiable as a realist theory of meaning for the reason that truth and truth-conditions both serve the purpose of establishing the fact that meaning and meaning-relations are real and are independent of the cognizers of meaning. The realism of this kind is defined as the doctrine that holds that truth and meaning are independent of the users of language, that is, they are cognition-independent in the sense that truth remains as it is even if there is no cognizer of it.[20] This characterization of meaning in terms of truth-conditions does presuppose that truth is a fundamental concept and that, as a semantic category, it is not epistemically derived from the way we know the truth of the sentences. That is why it is held that truth-conditions are the conditions under which the sentences are true or false and not the conditions under which we come to know them as true or false.

There are two assumptions which the realist is bound to make:

1. The truth-conditions are derivable in a Tarskian way, that is, in the way a truth-schema is available in a logical language. The truth-schema is of the following kind, namely,

    S is true iff *p*.

    Here *p* stands for the sentence itself whereas S is the name of the sentence or the sentence in quotation. This condition is logically necessary since here it is imperative that truth-conditions need a metalanguage for their expression.

2. The truth-conditions are determinate since there is nothing here that can cause indeterminacy. For example, there is transparency as regards the necessity of the truth-formula and there is no ambiguity as regards the fact that truth-conditions are available for every well-formed sentence.

Both these conditions go a long way towards establishing that truth-conditions are a part of the semantic strategy that explains meaning in the logico-semantic tradition.

The question is, what sort of realism is involved here and whether such a realism is warranted at all? The realism that is involved is that it takes for granted a concept of truth that fits into the classical concept of correspondence. This is the concept that shows that the truth of a sentence follows from the fact that the world exists independently of us and that language is a representation of the world. That is to say, the world is an independent existence and that language is logically linked with the former in such a way that our sentences are bound to be true or false. This is called the principle of bivalence.[21] This principle is the very foundation of two-valued logic and semantics, and that accounts for the fact that any theory of truth must take note of the fact that truth-conditions are logically linked with the meaning of the sentences.

The immediate consequence for the meaning theory is that truth-conditions logically follow from the meaning of the sentences. Suppose we are in need of telling another speaker of English that "Snow is white" and that, for both of us, this sentence is meaningful. Then the immediate question is, what do we mean by the meaning of this sentence? In whatever way we explain the meaning of this sentence, it is found to be true in our world and so we know that this sentence is both meaningful and true. But that is not enough. The sentence could have been false under some other conditions. The logical structure of the sentence shows that the sentence is either true or false and that its meaning has something to do with these facts about its truth or falsity. Thus there is interdependence between truth and meaning in the sense that, wherever there is meaning, there is truth or falsity. Meaning is the other logical feature of a sentence that has truth-possibility. Thus in logical semantics there is a logical trade-off between truth and meaning.

The field theory of language takes it as *prima facie* acceptable that, language being a representation of the world, it is inevitable that sentences are either true or false. So there is no reason to believe that language could ever in theory be without the concept of truth. The fields we have talked about are the fields that make representations either true or false. But this does not imply that meaning is derived from truth or that it is explicable only in terms of truth-conditions. Meaning is collateral with truth-conditions but is not identical with the latter. Here our theory differs from the Davidsonian theory that truth-conditions alone account for meaning or that truth-conditions and meaning are the same semantic reality. The reason for this view is that truth-conditions follow from meaning and not the other way round. If truth-conditions make meaning possible, then what will happen to those sentences which do not have recognizable truth-conditions? Besides, what will happen to the sentences which are not meant as descriptions of the world? These questions will be raised later while discussing the anti-realist theory of language and meaning. But, for the time being, it can be shown that there is *prima facie* reason why truth-conditions cannot be taken as meaning itself. This view is a semantically reductionist programme since it reduces meaning to the truth-conditions themselves. Semantic reductionism does not hold good especially when truth-conditions are available only for the descriptions of world.

The following are the two accounts of truth-conditions in language — the stronger one of holding that truth-conditions and meaning are the same and the weaker one of holding that meaning and truth-conditions are logically linked. The latter thesis holds good for the large part of the field of language. Language being the field of representations it is logically sound to hold that truth and meaning are semantically co-present in the structure of language. No account of the field of language is possible if truth is not presupposed as a basic category. But that already presupposes that language is meaningful in the sense that we have already an account of the sense and force of the sentences of that language.

Anti-Realism and the Fate of Truth-Conditions

Anti-realism comes forward to account for meaning in a non-truth-condition way. It holds that meaning is a matter of the language being in use and therefore being constantly in the commerce of life. So there is a logical relation of meaning with use and the conditions under which language is used. As Dummett[22] has shown, there is a direct link between the meaning of the sentence and its assertion-conditions, that is, the conditions under which the sentence is being used, that is, asserted or denied. Thus anti-realism tells the story of meaning without taking into account the truth-conditions as the logical semanticists wanted to have them as the foundations of meaning. A new foundation is being searched for meaning within language itself.

The new foundations are located within the realm of the language-use or what is otherwise known as the assertion-environment of the sentences. That is to say, the new understanding of meaning lies in how the sentences are themselves made to function within the realm of life and the world. The later Wittgenstein has shown the way how to locate the meaning in the realm of the language-games and the forms of life.[23] This focuses on what can be construed as the use-approach or the functional approach to meaning. It introduces the dimension of time and the axis of life in the semantic considerations of meaning. The time-dimension refers to the fact that use of language is bound to the historical conditions and the so-called surroundings as Wittgenstein used to say. These historical surroundings include the fact that language is part of the natural history of man.[24] This shows that meaning considerations are such that they include the necessary conditions of how language comes to be used in a regular and grammatical fashion. The fact of language-use is necessary fact in that without it we cannot conceive of language as rule-following behaviour of mankind. It is therefore inevitable that the life-axis comes into operation as the metaphysical background of meaning. Meanings are the normative structures of the forms of life. A form of life, for that matter, is not an accidental feature of language and therefore, in order that language and life are regular patterns of existence, meaning must arise as the normative structure. Thus there is a significant link between meaning and life so far as language and life go together.

If this is a movement towards anti-realism as it is supposed to be the case by Dummett[25] and Wright,[26] then it can mean that meaning is not a metaphysical entity that can be grasped as a

Fregean sense. It is, contrarily, to be taken as a human construction and, if necessary, as a human convention. This way of approaching meaning is embedded in the anti-realistic framework itself. According to this framework, the conditions of meaning are not independent of the the language-use and the participants in the language-games. Meaning is rather a product of the interaction of man and language and it is mostly a matter of how man participates in language and not how language itself embodies meaning. The latter is jettisoned as the relic of the realist doctrine of meaning. If meaning is the man-independent grammatical reality, then, it is argued, meaning becomes a transcendent reality and thus ceases to be relevant to man. Therefore anti-realism argues that meaning is immanent to the linguistic activities and the forms of life and not transcendent to language and life.

The greatest challenge of anti-realism is against the realist notion of truth and truth-conditions. For it, the realist notion of truth bears the stigma of transcendence as truth, defined as correspondence, presupposes that a sentence is true even if there is nobody to cognize that it is true. Besides, the sentence is made true by the world which stands independently of us. Thus the world is the ultimate horizon of truth that stands above the contingent stream of life and language. This commitment to the transcendent reality of the world makes truth equally a transcendent notion such that the language-use and the forms of life are only contingent realizations of the former. Realism thus allegedly makes language accidental to truth and meaning in the sense that the sentences are man-made instruments which are supposed to realize the meaning and truth-conditions already present in the semantic realm.

Anti-realism stands opposed to the transcendent notion of meaning and truth. It argues that meaning is the matter of language-use or the assertions of the sentences and their availability in the entire repertoire of linguistic activities. These are summarily called the 'assertion-conditions' which make for the meaning of the sentences. The assertion-conditions are the other name for the conditions under which the assertions are made. The assertions are made in the network of language-games and so there is a link between how the assertions are made and their possible conditions of being true or false. Thus meaning is now a complex product of the assertability-conditions and their possible truth-values. The anti-realist does not hold that truth is irrelevant to meaning or that it is accidental to language. Rather, for him, the meaning is the joint product of the pro-attitude of the language-user and the positive response of the world. If the world continues to be language-indifferent and so irrelevant to truth, then there would be no meaning at all in language since we can never use it in the world. Language-use presupposes the constancy in the world and also the responsiveness of the latter to language. Thus it is ontologically necessary that truth and meaning are not totally dissociated in anti-realism.

But anti-realism does stand for the idea that truth cannot be independent of our mind. If truth is independent of our mind, then it will lead to the irrelevance of truth itself and thus there would be no ground on which truth can be semantically necessary. The semantic necessity of truth lies in the fact that language represents the world. Anti-realism safeguards the necessity of truth by telling that truth is immanent rather than transcendent and so there is no reason to believe that truth will disappear under the new scheme of assertibility-conditions. Dummett appears to make truth a verificational category such that, wherever verification is possible, truth is possible and *vice versa*. This leads to the supposition that truth and verification together make meaning possible.[27] However, Dummett distances himself from a clear-cut demarcation of truth in terms of verification because, for him, the principle of bivalence does not ultimately work and so it is not necessary that all sentences when verified will yield truth or falsity. All that is required by him is the fact that truth follows only in those cases where meaning is otherwise guaranteed. That is, only in those cases where meaning is part of the use-frame of the sentence there is likelihood of truth emerging if the sentence is a description of the world. If the sentence is non-assertorial, then the verification of the sentence within a finite time is not possible and there is no question of its being true or false. It is necessary that truth fails in the non-representational case, but meaning remains all the more secure as a paradigm case of truth-resistance. Dummett puts a constraint on all verifications and that is the finite time constraint which says that a sentence to be verified requires to be so within a finite stretch of time.[28] This finitist demand is meant only for truth and not for meaning as meaning does not lie within the finite time-frame. Truth, according to Dummett, is a finite notion and so it cannot be the basis for the non-finitist notion of meaning. In this framework truth and meaning are separated for the reason that meaning is open to verification across time but truth is so open only for the finitist framework. This may mean that anti-realism has made room for two frameworks — one for truth and one for meaning and thus rejects the realist's amalgamation of the two.

For the anti-realist, the correspondence view of truth is an anachronism as it has lost the very meaning it had in the classical tradition. First of all, it has lost its honorific title as it is no more transcendent and secondly, it has lost the capacity to spread across time. Again it does not apply to all sectors of language as language is not truth-functional throughout. So, truth-conditional semantics failing, it is necessary that a new semantics of assertions and assertability-conditions be accepted. This fits in with Dummett's proposal for intuitionist logic and semantics which assures of the constructibilty of meaning and truth.[29]

The anti-realist theory of meaning follows as a corollary of the new semantics of assertions in the intuitionist framework. The meaning theory aims at the understanding of meaning as a datum of empirical experience. The anti-realists are united on the fact that meaning is cognitively grasped and that it is available to the semantic framework. This results in the fact that meaning is no more a matter of positing a meaning-essence but it is one of constituting a meaning-frame that accommodates the fact of language-use, convention-setting and also the possibility of verification. The latter component is the one of making available the framework of language to public grasp and public mastery. Language has the ability to be mastered as the totality of the speech-phenomena and thus it becomes a part of the life of the community. Dummett amongst others finds that language-mastery is the method of understanding meaning and so must be placed within the semantic strategy of providing assertability-conditions of the sentences.

The question, however, remains as to how meaning can be a matter of practice and mastery if the concept of meaning is not already presupposed by the framework of language-use. Wittgenstein has not made clear whether meaning precedes language-use or not. If meaning follows language-use, then it is difficult to account for the regularity and necessity in language-use. Again, if meaning precedes language-use, one wonders in what way the latter can explain meaning. These difficulties are not solved by Dummett. He takes for granted that meaning is a matter of linguistic practice without telling how it can enter into practice without being a pre-language-use concept. If meaning shows sign of being a pre-theoretical notion, then it is imperative that we go beyond the anti-realist framework for a better understanding of the concept of meaning.

From Anti-Realism to Internal Realism

The primacy of the truth-conditions being denied in anti-realism, there is little scope for a meaning theory to reinstate them in their original form. The anti-realist critique of the classical notion of truth has come to stay in spite of the obvious difficulties associated with it. Yet Putnam[30] has tried his best to provide an alternative to the meaning realism in his internalist framework. Meaning realism in the classical form adhering to the primacy of truth has been, rather, rejected and in its place a new concept of internal realism has been established. The central thesis of internal realism in meaning theory is that meaning is not centrally dependent on the correspondence theory of truth. Rather than meaning being dependent on truth, truth is now found to be closely following meaning. It is thereby held that meaning is a matter of how we organize our language and its representations rather than of how the language is about the world in a metaphysical and transcendental sense. Putnam has been a consistent critic of the transcendent and the God's-point-of-view theory of truth and meaning. This has led him to view meaning as a matter of the use and the organized practice of language.

According to Putnam, the transcendent point of view takes a highly metaphysical view of language and the world. The realist, for example, believes that language represents the world in such a way that these representations are all independent of how we learn the language and use it according to the set norms. For the realist, the representations are either true or false from a God's Eye point of view.[31] That is, they are true or false independently of the concepts and categories of the people who make the representations. This therefore results in the fact that truth is taken as the bedrock of the metaphysics of language and the world. Meaning accordingly is defined as the metaphysical content of language that is ontologically there independently of us.

This metaphysical view of the functioning of language and meaning is repugnant to the internal realist who can see that truth and meaning are really rooted in the conceptual framework that underlies our language and thought. Putnam, for instance, finds that truth cannot operate as a semantic category unless we introduce language-use as a primary datum. Only in a language setting, where the division of linguistic labour holds good, there can be talk of reference and truth.[32] To refer is to causally associate the word with the object and thus there is an established mechanism through which we can accomplish this. This cannot be left to the arbitrary whim of the referring person nor to the magical operation of a machine. Thus language has to evolve both exit and entry rules for this purpose. This will settle the question of reference and truth in a more acceptable sense as both these concepts are semantically so important.

But the main point for the internal realist is that neither truth nor reference can be made external to the conceptual system that we possess. This conceptual system is the one we inherit and work with so far as our conception of the world is concerned. It is the basic point of departure for all our thought and language. Given this scheme of thought and things, it is necessary that we can judge whether we can refer to the world successfully or not only within this scheme. Our success or failure is conditioned by the world-picture that we have. Besides, there is nothing that is called the world as such since the so-called world-in-itself is non-existent. The world that exists is the world that we can talk about and the world that we think through our concepts. The world is, in a sense, our world, that is, the world that we have structured through our concepts. This world is fully transparent to our conceptual network such that the truth we can talk of is the one we have participated in. That is, truth and world are both internal to our language and conceptual scheme, and so there is no God's Eye view of things. The latter view is cancelled because we cannot go beyond our system of categories to view the things as it were from above.

Putnam defines truth as the rational acceptability[33] of the knowledge-claims that we make since therein lies the possibility of evaluating these claims according to the standards accepted for the purpose. The standards are the ones which are accepted after deliberate decision rationally undertaken by the community of thinkers. The rational community of thinkers together makes the move regarding what to accept as true or false in a certain context. Thus truth is internalized to the scheme of things and the norms set for the purpose of evaluation. The result is the fact that all of us are responsible for the truth or falsity of the knowledge-claims made.

In this context, what is meaningful for the rational community of language-users is what is openly canvassed as meaning in that context. For example, whether a sentence is meaningful or not does not depend entirely on what it represents but on what is judged as representing at all. That is, before we could tell what is a true representation, we must have decided what is called representation at all. Then only we can say that a sentence is true or false about the world. This requires a primitive concept of being about the world. That cannot be derived from language since language is the very notion of representation. Putnam therefore goes back to the community to find out what is called our being about the world. The rational community is so made that all of them talk about the world in their language and so there is a consensus on this issue. Language is representational because of this community sanction.

The meaning relations that govern our language are all nested in the network of the rational decisions of the community. Thus meaning emerges as a socially evolved mass of norms and rules all put into the network of language. Internal realism faces the problem of meaning rather squarely as a datum of the ongoing business of language and the community reactions. Here is the crucial choice for the internal realist. Either he accepts meaning as given in language or he takes meaning as man-made. If he accepts the first alternative, he has to accept an unrepentant kind of realism about meaning. If he accepts the second alternative, he finds himself in the company of the relativists who make meaning a matter of accepted conventions. Both alternatives are unwelcome. The internal realist is enough of a realist to understand that realism though true cannot be of the exteranlist type, that is, that it cannot take meaning as a transcendent notion. Secondly, he is enough of an internalist to take meaning as a subjective entity at all. At least, Putnam understands that subjectivism is self-defeating,[34] as any other such absurd-looking doctrine is. Hence the right attitude of the internal realist is to take meaning as the rationally acceptable sets of norms and concepts that govern the use of language. Meaning, no doubt, is a matter of social practice but that does not rule out the fact that meaning is normative and so is not arbitrary and whimsical in its structure.

Can, then, the internalist meaning theory plug the loopholes in the semantics of consensus and rational choice? There are many aspects to this problem. First, the idea of rational consensus is not very clear such that it can bear the burden of the semantic meaning. This is because what is rationally decided by the community itself presupposes that there is language and meaning. Meaning cannot come into existence by virtue of agreement since in agreeing over an issue we have already taken language as meaningful. Secondly, the rational consensus is rather a vague concept as it does not tell what are the criteria which decide what is rational. The search for criteria of rationality leads to circularity as rational is that which is based on the criteria and the criteria are those that are rationally decided and so on. Thus there arises the need to accept something as basic and fundamental in this context. If meaning itself is reduced to a set of norms, then the norms must be fundamental and so there is no need to go beyond them to find out the source of the norms themselves. But this does not solve the problem since, decidedly, norms require a language which is already meaningful. Putnam is thus compelled to concede that meaning is itself fundamental though we can provide explanation of meaning in terms of the language-use and the community sanctions. Certain idealized conditions are imposed on our language-use and thus there is a safer way of ensuring that meaning is an internal feature of our language.

Internal realism succeeds to a great extent in freeing meaning from the contentious metaphysical issues like the independence of meaning from the language-user and also its dependence on truth and reference. Meaning is not a matter of reference though truth is. That is why truth and meaning are independent of each other. In spite of this rather innocuous discovery, it does not follow that truth does not matter for language or that language is not representational. Putnam agrees with Dummett and Davidson that language represents the world and that language has in-built truth-conditions. But it is another matter that meaning is not defined in terms of truth-conditions. From the representational point of view, meaning and truth come in a semantic package though meaning is the primary desideratum.

The Unified Theory

The proposal for a unified theory is forthcoming in view of the fact that meaning and truth form a compact set of concepts in semantics. There are two reasons why a unified theory forces itself on us. First, truth is not an anathema to meaning as every true sentence must be meaningful and *vice versa*. It was not a mistake that Frege called truth a primitive concept in language. He equally emphasized that sense is a fundamental notion. Both these concepts are co-present in language. Second, meaning or sense is such that we cannot detach it from truth since all meaningful language is also either true or false, or it is linked with the language already known to be true or false. Lastly, in a system of language as representations of the world the twin concepts of truth and meaning are co-present. So the theory of meaning must be such that it can do full justice to the concepts of truth and meaning and other related concepts.

The first step of the unified theory is to suggest that meaning is a representational concept. This is not to say that meaning is referential in the crude sense. Representestations are what language does in its multifaceted structure. A representation is a way of telling what the world is and this is the rudimentary function of language as we have argued so far. This function derives not from how language is empirically structured but from its logical form. That is to say that language logically represents the world. If this thesis holds, then the anti-representationalist[35] cannot argue that language only partially does this function or does not do it at all. This view is derived from the thesis that language is a form of life and action rather than of representing something standing outside. Those who say with Dewey, Heidegger and the later Wittgenstein that language is the system of life's manifold business are of the opinion that, for these philosophers, language ceases to be a mirror of the universe.[36] Instead, language becomes a non-representational way of disclosing the reality in many-faceted ways. Even if this view is otherwise correct, it cannot establish that language does not say anything about the world. It is almost impossible to detach language from the world. Whether there is representational relation between language and the world is a matter of debate but it is not debatable that language and the world are related. If it can be shown that language is indifferent to the world, then it goes without saying that language is not even a form of life or even not the home of Being in Heidegger's sense. Language, in this sense, may mean many things to non-representationalist. It may mean just a set of symbols or a set of activities or even a mass of syntactic structures. But in all these the assumption is that language does something fundamental regarding the world. It reveals the world and discloses its inner structure. The Being in fact is revealed in the linguistic structure itself. This is a representational concept in that language and Being are interdependent in their ultimate structure.

The unified theory makes a reconciliation of the two approaches to language, namely, the anti-realist and the anti-representationalist theory, on the one hand, and the realist and the representationalist theory, on the other. It accepts the view that truth and meaning are internal to the language and the conceptual system and that there is no transcendent[37] vantage point from which we can evaluate the truth-claims themselves. Thus there is, admittedly, truth in the internalist and anti-realist point of view. But that does not mean that realism as such is dead. Realism of the metaphysical type cannot hold good because it makes extravagant claims about the nature of the world and the relationship between language and the world. So it is necessary that we soften the stand of the realist to realize that language is, after all, a human institution and that it is historically conditioned in many ways. Given these conditions in which man and his language operate, there is room for doubt as to whether language and the world can be related without a trace of human intervention.

The historicality of language and man does not spell disaster for semantics and logic since there is still the talk of a meaning theory that makes meaning a non-contingent concept in semantics. Meaning is the domain of language that speaks of its inner structure, rules and norms that define how language itself functions. So the idea of the functions of language must presuppose that there is a way of its functioning. That way is precisely the meaning that remains the desideratum of language.

The main question is, how do we account for meaning? The accounting is variable though meaning remains invariant. The ways of meaning are many in the sense that there are different routes to the meaning available. But it does not mean that there are many meanings in the same system for the same expression. The methods of explanation, realist or non-realist, may differ as the approaches to the reality are always different. But meaning itself is the invariant core of language. Language holds its core to itself as it is its inner essence and it is its grammatical form. In that sense meaning is the bedrock of language and so must be seen as such. Truth follows language as its metaphysical shadow and so there is no denying that meaning leads to the possibility of truth itself.

To conclude: it is the unified meaning theory that can ensure that meaning is not a contingent concept in language and that it is neither the truth-conditions nor the justification-conditions alone which can guarantee meaning. Meaning is already given in language and that alone can tell what a truth-condition or a justification-condition can mean. Thus semantics must look into language to discover the meaning. Meaning speaks for itself.

References

1. The concept of field of language stands for the system of language. It is closer to Wittgenstein's concept of language-game. A field of language is the space of linguistic activities. *See* Wittgenstein, *Zettel* (Blackwell, Oxford, 1967), sect. 43.

2. Frege, *The Foundations of Arithmetic*, tr. by J.L. Austin (Blackwell, Oxford, 1950).

3. Frege, "On Sense and Reference" in *Translations from the Philosophical Writings of Gottlob Frege*, tr. by P.T. Geach and M. Black (Blackwell, Oxford, 1952).

4. Wittgenstein, *Tractatus Logico-Philosophicus*, tr. by D.F. Pears and B.F. McGuinness (Routledge and Kegan Paul, London, 1961), 4.022.

5. *See* Donald Davidson, "Truth and Meaning", in *Inquiries into Truth and Interpretation* (Clarendon Press, Oxford, 1984), pp. 17-35.

6. Davidson, "Belief and the Basis of Meaning", in *Inquiries into Truth and Interpretation*, pp. 141-53.

7. Cf. Henry Staten, *Wittgenstein and Derrida*, (Blackwell, Oxford, 1984) Chapters 1 and 2.

8. *Ibid.*

9. E. Cassirer, *The Philosophy of Symbolic Forms* vol. I, tr. by R. Manheim (Yale University Press, New Haven, 1955).

10. *See* Husserl, *Ideas: General Introduction to Pure Phenomenology*, tr. by W.R. Boyce Gibson (Allen and Unwin, London, 1931).

11. For an account of ineffable semantics *see*, Hintikka and

Hintikka, *Investigating Wittgenstein*, (Blackwell, Oxford,1986).

12.   *See* J.L. Austin, *How to Do Things with Words* (Harvard University Press, Cambridge, Mass., 1962).

13.   *Ibid. See* J.R. Searle, *Speech-Acts* (Cambridge University Press, Cambridge, 1962).

14.   *Ibid.*

15.   *See* H.P. Grice, "Meaning", in *Philosophical Review*, 66 (1957), 377-88. *See also* P.F. Strawson, "Intention and Convention in Speech Acts", in *Logico-Linguistic Papers* (Methuen, London,1971).

16.   Cf. F. Recanati, *Meaning and Force*, (Cambridge University Press, Cambridge,1987).

17.   R. Carnap, *Introduction to Semantics* (Harvard University Press, Cambridge, Mass.,1942).

18.   Wittgenstein, *Tractatus Logico-Philosophicus*, 4.024.

19.   Cf. Davidson, "Truth and Meaning", in *Inquiries into Truth and Interpretation*, pp.3-36.

20.   Michael Dummett, "What is a Theory of Meaning?", in *Mind and Language*, ed. by S. Guttenplan (Clarendon Press, Oxford, 1975). *See also* his "What is Theory of Meaning? II", in *Meaning and Truth* ed. by Evans and McDowell (Clarendon Press, Oxford, 1976).

21.   *Ibid.*

22.   *Ibid.*

23.   Wittgenstein, *Philosophical Investigations*, tr. by Anscombe (Blackwell, Oxford, 1953) sect. 23.

24.   *Ibid.* sect. 25.

25.   Dummett, "Truth", in *Philosophical Logic*, ed. by P.F. Strawson, Oxford University Press, Oxford, 1967).

26.   C. Wright, *Wittgenstein on the Foundations of Mathematics*, (Duckworth, London,1980).

27.   *Ibid.*

28.   Cf. Dummett, "Truth", in *Philosophical Logic*, ed. by P.F. Strawson.

29. Dummett, "What is a Theory of Meaning? II", in *Meaning and Truth*, ed. by Evans and McDowell.

30. *See* Putnam, *Reason, Truth and History*, (Cambridge University Press, Cambridge, 1981).

31. *Ibid.*, pp. 49-50.

32. *Ibid.*, pp. 22-48.

33. *Ibid.*, pp. 54-56.

34. *Ibid.*

35. R. Rorty, "Representation, Social Practise and Truth", in *Objectivity, Relativism and Truth* (Cambridge University Press, Cambridge, 1991).

36. Rorty, *Philosophy and the Mirror of Nature* (Princeton Univerity Press, Princeton, 1979).

37. W. V. Quine, *Word and Object* (MIT Press, Cambridge, Mass., 1960).

6

Semantics Denaturalized

In this chapter we shall delineate the structure of semantics that can validate the representational theory of meaning we have so far argued for. Two problems come to notice which need immediate attention: they are (1) the problem of naturalism in semantics and (2) the problem of validating a meaning theory against the sceptical attack on the idea of meaning itself. Both these problems have been bothering the semanticists of our times. Quine, for example, has himself raised these questions with regard to meaning and language and has come out with a solution that verges on naturalism and scepticism. It is Quine who has awakened us to the dangers of transcendent and *a priori* semantics which has allegedly posed an impasse in meaning theory by reducing meaning to an extra-mental and extra-terrestrial entity in a Platonic world. This, according to Quine, is an untenable position in philosophy of language. In this chapter we shall argue that Quine's naturalism itself leads to meaning-scepticism and so we must not give up the *a priori* semantics as such. We should rather found semantics on the firmer grounds that can ensure meaning and truth in language and can sufficiently invalidate scepticism.

The main contention of this chapter is that semantics is an

autonomous discipline and that it is capable of explaining meaning without reducing it either to mental content or to the set of stimulus and response of the speech-community. Meaning is the very content of language that represents the world. Therefore meaning lies in the representationality of language.

Semantic Naturalism

Semantic naturalism is the theory that both language and meaning are natural facts of man's linguistic behaviour and are thus part of the natural world. That is to say that language is a natural phenomenon and so must be seen as belonging to the domain of the natural facts such as the facts in the world of empirical experience. Viewed in this way, language can cease to appear as anything other than the domain of the facts relating to what language does as a communicational and social institution. John Dewey in his *Experience and Nature*[1] made the far reaching claim that language is basically a social institution and that its function is to facilitate communication and the related human activities. Therefore there is a naturalness about language and so it must be scientifically studied in order to understand its meaning. Dewey's main effort is to bring language back into the fold of human activities and life in general and to see if it can be studied as one of the very important facts of human life. In this sense, he has anticipated the development of the naturalistic view of language and meaning that has broadly taken language as an evolving phenomenon of human life in the natural world. In this view meaning, which is the very essence of language, is taken as the cumulative set of rules and norms that evolve though time and which endow the human activities with a stable and universal sense.[2]

Dewey's naturalistic view of language and meaning is echoed in Quine's theory of language which goes more radical so far as making language a natural set of activities is concerned. Quine makes language a natural sort of behaviour that man uniquely inherits from his biological ancestry. The biological past of man stands as the background of the enormous complexity of the linguistic behavoiur of man. That is the reason Quine thinks that language and meaning are part of the behaviour of man.[3] According to Quine, language has two main features, namely, its surface feature of being a network of stimulus and response, that is, being an effective medium of communication among the human beings, and its depth-structure being one of a standard logical grammar of the truth-functional type. The latter feature is the universal feature of all human languages and therefore there is the possibility of developing a logical grammar for language.[4] Quine's theory, however, is known for the other feature that brings language back into the natural world. That is the feature of language as a set of activities of the behavioural type. This is highlighted in the literature as it tells how Quine took the naturalistic turn in philosophy of language.

The naturalistic turn consists in making language less a matter of *a priori* grammar but more a matter of the natural world which indicates that the linguistic rules and the meaning of the linguistic expressions all evolve through a natural process. The natural processes are of the type of causal and deterministic structures such that an empirical science of those structures is possible. In this sense a science of language and meaning is possible that tells how the semantic relations have evolved in time and also how the meanings have come into existence as a part of the social life of the people concerned. According to Quine, language is a social institution[5] and it is more a communicational device than a sort of logical structure. Hence the emphasis on the natural evolution of language and meaning.

Given the above-mentioned features of language, it can be said that the naturalistic turn in philosophy of language has been significant for the following reasons:

1. It has shown that language cannot be taken in the metaphysical sense as a museum piece in that it is

something ideal and removed from the practical contingencies of human life.

2. It has also shown that meaning is not an ideal entity either in the Fregean Third World or in the mind of the people.

These two theses are basic to Quine's naturalistic semantics. The first thesis tells that the natural language is the language that is real and it is the one we are concerned with in actual life. The so-called ideal languages are either linguistic myths or the creations of the idle logical mind. This makes Quine the important spokesman of naturalism in semantics and metaphysics. The second thesis is the one that makes meaning a social reality rather than a reality of the metaphysical kind. Thus naturalism makes an important departure from classical semantics and metaphysics.

The Facts of the Matter

Quine makes a pointed inquiry into what it is that constitutes the facts of the matter in semantics. His interest in the facts of the matter lies in his important discovery that there is no fact of the matter[6] in semantics in the classical sense. That is to say that the classical semantic theory that mentions the necessities, rules and meanings as the basic facts of the matter is really mistaken as these categories themselves cannot be explained without circularity.[7] The concepts of the classical logic and semantics which involve the analytic truths fail to sustain themselves as they cannot explain how the analytic-synthetic distinction can be maintained at all. Thus Quine concludes that the classical semantic theory must be based on a mistake.[8]

The mistake lies in the classical theory of meaning itself which Frege and Carnap, among others, held to be true. The theory is like this: meaning is an ideal entity and it is of the character of a logical object. This is what Frege called sense (*sinn*) and Carnap called intension. In either sense it is a logico-linguistic entity that remains as it is independently of language-use. Such an entity is a myth, according to Quine. That is why he calls for the rejection of this theory of meaning itself. According to him, a naturalized semantics must replace the classical theory such that now semantics becomes the science of the speech behaviour and that the key to meaning lies in the sense-experience that lies at the foundation of semantics and epistemology.[9]

The collapse of the classical theory results in the loss of determinacy of meaning and reference and thus in what Quine calls the indeterminacy of translation.[10] The first loss is the loss of determinacy which is the cornerstone of classical semantics. This signalizes the fact that meaning becomes an indeterminate concept as there is nothing that can be called the meaning of an expression. The expression could, under varying circumstances, take different meanings depending upon the context and the speech-situation. This itself makes room for the inscrutability of reference of the expression as well. The latter follows as a matter of course, since there is nothing to determine what is the real referent of a term like 'gavagai' in the native language.[11] What is true of a native language expression is also true of all expressions: they simply do not have absolutely determinate referents. Thus classical semantics is almost rejected as a result of the collapse of the idea of semantic determinacy.

However, according to Quine, the most significant development in naturalized semantics is the emergence of indeterminacy of translation. It has been held that two languages can be inter-tanslated without a shade of indeterminacy because it is assumed that there is meaning which is invariant across languages. This blind acceptance of meaning as an invariant entity leads to the false idea that languages are intertanslated. But naturalized semantics shows that this is not possible. The sentence could be variously translated if different analytic hypotheses[12] are available.

This possibility arises because there are, in fact, various such hypotheses which a speech-community may evolve. There is, indeed, no limit to the natural interpretations of human speech and there is no one way in which language can be understood. Hence the idea of indeterminacy of translation.

Semantics Needs Foundations

Although the determinacy of meaning and translations is seen to be collapsing in the naturalized semantics, yet it remains the case that semantics as such needs foundations of its own. This is so because there is a need to ground the semantic structures of language in the language itself. If language has no structures of the needed sort, even meaning will not be possible. Quine realizes this in his effort to see that language has a grammar[13] and that there is a logical format for all language analysis. This is further developed in the theory that language has a logical structure that can be captured in a first-order logic. This is the foundation that language needs for its being meaningful and true at all. Like Frege, Quine is assured of the fact that language has both truth and meaning as the semantic features and so there must be a grounding of these concepts in language. This grounding is possible if there is a semantic structure available along with the logical structure of language. In view of this, it is quite logical to believe that semantics is still in need of a solid foundation in the structure of language.

To a great extent, Quine tries to make semantics logical because he believes that semantics is basically a logical study of language. Even then, he is aware that semantics is an empirical study of language. That is why he has made semantics a part of the science of language and human behaviour. The important thing, for Quine, is the fact that language is a behavioural phenomenon and that the ultimate foundation of the study of language is the behavioural dispositions and other allied implicit or explicit physical properties of the speech community. Thus a semanticist is a natural scientist in that he studies the linguistic phenomena as the empirical data.[14] Thus, in.Quine, there is an amalgamation of logic and empirical science both aiming at the establishment of a science of semantics.

But now the question is: in what sense has Quine succeeded in providing a foundation for semantics? Apparently, he has, rather, failed in providing any foundation for the semantic study of language and meaning. All that he has done is that he has taken a radical turn towards making semantics an empirical discipline. He has brought semantics into the fold of natural science and has rejected the so-called transcendental study of language and meaning. According to him, the first philosophy[15] of language and meaning is not available since there is no way of studying language by going beyond language. Besides, the so-called meaning as an ideal entity itself cannot be sustained in view of the fact that meanings are not non-natural entities of any sort. Thus there is, in fact, a denial of foundations for semantics and so it has been Quine's oft-repeated slogan that meanings are simply dead and there need be no more any search for them.

But, as we know, this radical thesis does not simply hold good, not only for the fact that language is still a systematic structure of meanings, rules and grammatical entities, but also for the fact that there is always a definite way we can bring out the semantic structure of language. That shows that there are facts of the matter so far as semantics is concerned. These facts consist in the availability of determinacy of meaning and reference in our natural languages. For instance, it is an admitted fact that whenever we speak a language we have determinate conception of what we are saying. It is not that every time there is a speech phenomenon we have to ask the semanticist whether there is meaning in the speech or not. We do not bother whether there is any indeterminacy in what we are saying. The hearer, as much as the speaker, is assured of the fact that there is meaning in what we say and also there is certainty in what we mean. The naturalist is unwarrantedly worrying over the fact that the indeterminacy is so rampant that we cannot really be sure of anything in our language-use. Wittgentein, for example, has called such worries the result of a philosophical misunderstanding of language and meaning. If it is admitted that meaning is what language does in the actual transactions of life, there is no reason to believe that we are all the time losing our grip over it in language-use. This scepticism regarding meaning-determinacy is out of question as it is illogical to deny the obvious fact that there is meaning in what we say in language as long as language is syntactically and semantically well-formed. Quine is unsure of the facts of meaning because he thinks that all meanings are, or must, be ideal entities.

Quine's attack on classical semantics is, rather, too radical because he forgets the fact that, even according to classical semantics, language need not entertain only ideal meanings. Even Frege never meant to suggest that meanings are such queer entities though he argued that meanings must be objective and stable unlike the so-called subjective apprehensions of meaning. Quine definitely agrees with Frege on this fact that even the empirical meaning, which the sentences have, must be objective and universal at least so far as that language is concerned. Quine has admitted that language must be related to experience and from that connection alone meaning follows. This indicates that meaning is intersubjective and real in the empirical sense. So empirical semantics must take note of the fact that meanings are there as part of language. The naturalist cannot deny that there are objective realities called semantic facts in language.

Besides, it does not behove the naturalist to say that empirical language lacks determinacy in meaning and reference. If that were the case, how can the language of science be at all determinate so that we can talk of the stimulus-meaning of the observation sentences at all? Even the theoretical sentences of science will lack meaning in the determinate sense and so there cannot be anything called science as a holistic structure. If Quine says that meaning of the theoretical sentences is only a matter of interpretation and there is enough relativist anchorage for science itself, then there is nothing to worry about the lack of determinacy of meaning. Meaning, after all, is available though only in the given context and in the framework in which it is raised.

The thesis of indeterminacy of translation underlines the fact that translations are context-based and are also open to revision. There is nothing called a universally acceptable translation of a language. So much is obvious and also a truism. If there is something more than this underlying the indeterminacy thesis, then it can be said that indeterminacy of the radical kind is itself a philosophical myth and need not be taken seriously. If languages are not intertranslatable in the normal sense, then there would be no communication and no transmission of knowledge from one language to another. Actual languages are all intertranslatable and so there is no place for scepticism regarding this possibility.

Against Naturalism

The real difficulty with Quine's theory of language and meaning is his naturalism. He has invited the naturalistic method of philosophizing for what he called eliminating the myth of museum of the classical theories of language. But, unfortunately, the same method has led him to overlook the merits of the classical philosophy. First of all, Quine has condemned what he called the first philosophy by which he meant the philosophy of the transcendental[16] kind. This is the refrain of his tirade against classical philosophy that the latter has really overstepped its limits in calling for a transcendental view of language and reality. The latter view consists in making the claim that there is a way of understanding language and meaning without taking into account the facts of language-use and that there is a method of telling what language is by going beyond language. The transcendental view is such that it transcends the factual details of language and considers them from outside of language. This way of putting the transcendental method, however, is not doing it justice at all. For example, Kant never meant to overlook the facts as such; in fact, he wanted to explain them though from an *a priori* angle. Frege also never meant to search for a metaphysical foundation for language and meaning. All that he did was to found language and meaning on logic and mathematics. So calling him a transcendentalist is not to understand him at all.

Naturalism as such is anti-metaphysical, though it itself is a metaphysics of its own type. It condemns anything and everything that goes beyond the experience of the sensuous kind. For such a philosophy there is nothing real except the empirical facts and their naturalistic meaning. So it is natural that it cannot understand how language can be understood *a priori* and so non-empirically. This is Quine's dilemma that though language is a natural fact, yet philosophy, which talks about it, is not natural in that sense. So there arises a gap between language and the philosophical activity of understanding language. The so-called first philosophy took the right view that there is a necessary gap between the two facts. It called the first fact the natural fact but it called the second the fact of the transcendental kind. That is why it called philosophy transcendental since the kind of things the latter does do not belong to the natural facts. Natural facts are given but the transcendental facts are not so given in sense-experience. So there is reason to take the latter differently. Quine, however, does the opposite by dissolving the distinction as such. He shows that the philosophical activity itself is nothing but a part of science[17] and so semantics, like logic, belongs to natural language and not to a domain beyond language.

If Quine's proposal is right, then the only activity possible will be science and nothing else. Philosophy, in that case, has no role to play except the one of collecting scientific data. In semantics it will mean it cannot raise the foundational question as such and so must reconcile to the role of making all meaning-questions irrelevant. This has been Quine's way out in solving the problem of meaning and reference. He comes closer to the view that, since philosophy in the old sense is dead, there is nothing that philosophy can do regarding meaning and reference. But in actual practice Quine has gone beyond that. He has raised questions about meaning and has like any other philosopher raised the foundational question and answered it, though negatively. He has gone to the extent of telling that meaning is not possible in the classical sense. Is this not a first philosophy as such? It is a first philosophy in the sense that it is telling something about language by going beyond language. Besides, it is telling that there is no meaning while presupposing that there is meaning in what it says. Thus Quine's own philosophy is as much a first philosophy as that of his opponents. This is the case because it is inevitable that, when we talk about meaning, we, though not removed from language, are still transcending the facts in the logical sense. No philosophy worth the name can remain indifferent to the claims of logically transcending the facts.

Quine is mistaken when he says that all talk about language and meaning is vitiated by the metaphysical presence of the ideal entities. This is true of some theories which trace out the meanings to their intensional origin in the mind. Quine is right in condemning mentalism as a theory of language and meaning. He is right in telling that, if meaning is a mental entity, it can easily be lost and its semantic identity dissolved. But, if meaning is identified with the sense-experience, there is the danger of losing meaning too, this time not inside mind but outside it. That is, there is no way of saving meaning even in the naturalistic scheme of things because there is nothing to distinguish meaning as a semantic entity from the experiential content or the stimulus-content. The latter is a physical fact and something belonging to the natural world but the former belongs, at least philosophically, to the realm of logic and semantics. Hence it can be argued that meaning and other semantic facts are not natural facts and must be in the logical space. Naturalism itself looks self-defeating as it carries forward its method to the very meaning it is presupposing.

Non-Naturalism and Semantic Facts

It is now a matter of universal acceptance that there are semantic facts concerning meaning and reference that cannot be explained naturalistically. The fact of the matter is that semantics offers facts of a very unique kind that are beyond the explanation of natural science. Such facts need an explanation that is not either psychologistic or physicalistic because they are not phenomena of either psychological or physical kind. They belong to a separate category, that is, the category of semantic facts. These facts are not reducible to any other facts since such a reduction can only distort them, not explain them properly. In this context, it is necessary to remember that Quine's attempt to reduce the semantic facts to the psycho-physical facts of the stimulus-response kind has failed since that led to the semantic indeterminacy of all kinds and ultimately made semantics a matter of behavioural psychology. This has led to the loss of semantic facts.[18]

It has been recognized that there are facts of the semantic kind which explain how meaning is possible and how language is semantically well-formed. This requires the reality of meaning as that set of semantic norms that are present in the very structure of language. Meanings are the facts of the normative kind that tell how a sentence or a group of sentences are meaningful and can at the same time function as the representations of the world. The most important fact in semantics is that which is about the representationality of language and that cannot be explained by some other fact, be it physical or mental. That is the reason why Putnam says that how a word or a sentence is meaningful is a fact that is based on the representational capacity of the latter to be related to the environment.[19] It is the interaction with the world that endows an expression with a semantic significance. This argument itself is not a physicalistic one as it presupposes that there is a deeper level of meaning that is beyond the physical facts. It is a transcendental argument, according to Putnam.[20] Similarly Katz argues that the semantic rules and structures of language together make up the semantic facts such that once we have a complete grasp of the facts we have a theory of semantics for that language. Thus semantic theory is a rational construction of language and the semantic facts such that we could postulate a metaphysics of meaning.[21]

What is implied by the above argument is that the semantic facts cannot easily be wished away because, if meaning is real, then there must be a definite method of explaining this fact. The explanation, though not always required, is after all possible in principle and this possibility is restated by the transcendental argument. The idea of transcendental argument, though not new, is of recent application in semantic theory. Frege anticipated it and Wittgenstein employed it with success for proving that if meaning is real then it must be so in the realm of grammar such that anybody who understands grammar of language cannot fail to see that meaning is the surest of the semantic facts.

The transcendental argument is committed to the fact that meaning can be described in a grammar though it cannot be constituted in the way the anti-realists claim. Meanings are as they are and not created for a purpose. That is, they are part of language and so describable in grammar. That is the reason they make their presence felt in the realm of use of language. The idea of semantic description suggests that there is a way to the semantic facts that does not lie through the mind or through the physical world. The semantic description is the linguistic representation of these facts in a grammatical medium. This is called the semantic description because there is no more interest in the reductivist programme of securing a place for semantics in the world of ideas or in the world of objects. Semantic description is the grammatical means of securing meaning and other semantic facts in an autonomous way.

The non-naturalism that we have talked about is the new requirement of providing semantic description in an autonomous way. It is forced on us because there is no way to semantic facts that goes through the natural facts. Natural facts are a necessary correlate of the semantic facts or the facts of language-use but the latter are not supervenient over the former. It is not necessary that semantic facts are explained by the natural facts and so there is a non-natural space for the semantic facts. The non-natural space is the one of meaning, norms and rules that is beyond the world of natural processes and events.[22]

Autonomy of Meaning and Semantic Theory

The inevitable consequence of the non-naturalistic standpoint is that we have to argue for the autonomy of meaning as it is evident that meaning, like other semantic facts, is embedded in an autonomous semantic space. The idea of autonomy is, rather, an old idea that demands that the demarcations of the concepts must be made clear. That is to say that we must aim at providing the grammar of the concepts in the appropriate sense. In this context, it is inevitable that meaning and other semantic concepts must be properly demarcated from other neighbouring concepts. This results in the autonomy principle.

So far as semantics is concerned the autonomy principle tells that there is a necessary gap between semantic theory and any other empirical theory of language. The semantic theory tells that language is a system of rules and structures of meaning that requires a new mode of introducing basic laws of language-formation. This theory may variously be articulated such as in truth-based semantics, verification model of semantics and the conceptual role semantics of the cognitivists,[23] etc. All these semantic theories presuppose that language is the basic principle of all semantic laws and relations. Language codifies the laws of semantics in a very determinate sense and so there can be a theory of semantics to uncover these laws.

The autonomy principle is forgotten, more often than not, in the semanticist's enthusiasm for a neat theory for articulating the semantic laws. It is forgotten that in the semantic theory itself the validity of semantics may be denied. This happens, for example, in the mental representation theories wherein the mental connections with the world are taken into account.[24] The mental representations do not explain themselves especially regarding their meaning and truth except in a language. Therefore it is required that language should be the solid bedrock of all activities, mental or otherwise. It is language alone that tells how a mental representation is meaningful. The mentalese[25] which is the language of the cognitive representations is very much a formal language that makes meaning and truth possible. So the apparent success of the mental representation theory as a theory of meaning underlines the fact that semantic facts need an autonomy of their own that goes beyond the domain of the mentalese itself. This is due to the fact that mental representations themselves are dependent on the linguistic representations. The linguistic representations are the primary semantic data that we take note of. Semantic theory is the theory of linguistic representations.

The question we have pursued so far is the one that concerns the linguistic representations themselves. These representations are the ones that concern not only the world but also our thoughts and their articulations in language. So there is a holistic sense in which representations are the very stuff of language, thought and our experience of the world. They constitute the core of language as a phenomenon in the human life and world. That signals the fact that language is constitutive of the human life-world.[26] It is because of this that language is an autonomous reality that reveals its meaning and truth in a unique sense. The

184 *Philosophy of Meaning and Representations*

semantic theory is the theory of how the autonomy of language and meaning can be secured while keeping in mind that meaning speaks of itself in language. The semantic theory is the theory of how language is itself not based on a theory.

References

1. **See** John Dewey, *Experience and Nature* (Oxford Book Company, Calcutta, 1965), Chapter V.

2. *Ibid.*

3. W.V. Quine, *Ontological Relativity and Other Essays* (Columbia University Press, New York, 1969), pp. 28-29.

4. Cf. Quine, *Philosophy of Logic* (Prentice-Hall Inc., Englewood Cliffs, N.J.,1970).

5. **See** Quine, *Methods of Logic* (Revised Edition, Holt, New York, 1959), Introduction.

6. **See** Quine, *Ontological Relativity and Other Essays*, pp. 30-67. **See also** his *Theories and Things* (Harvard Univerity Press, Cambridge, Mass., 1981), pp. 1-23.

7. Cf. Quine, "Two Dogmas of Empiricism", in *From a Logical Point of View* (Harvard University Press, Cambridge, Mass., 1953, Second Edition, 1980), pp. 20-46.

8. *Ibid.*

9. Quine, *Ontological Relativity and Other Essays*, pp. 89-90.

10. *Ibid.*, pp.30-67. **See also** *Word and Object* (MIT Press, Cambridge, Mass., 1960), Chapter II.

11. Cf. *Word and Object*, pp. 26-79.

12. *Ibid.*

13. **See** Quine, *Philosophy of Logic*.

14. Cf. *Word and Object*, Chapter II. **See also** Quine, "Mind and Verbal Dispositions", in *Mind and Language*, ed. by S. Guttenplan (Clarendon Press, Oxford, 1975), p. 91.

15. *Theories and Things*, pp. 22-23.

16. *Ibid.*

17.   Cf. "Two Dogmas of Empiricism", in *From a Logical Point of View*, pp. 20-36. **See also** *Word and Object*, pp. 270-76.

18.   Cf. *Ontological Relativity and Other Essays*, pp. 69-89.

19.   **See** Hilary Putnam,"The Meaning of 'Meaning'", in *Mind, Language and Reality* (Cambridge University Press, Cambidge, 1975), pp. 215-71.

20.   **See** Putnam, *Reason, Truth and History* (Cambridge University Press, Cambridge, 1981), pp. 49-74.

21.   **See** J.J. Katz, *Language and Other Abstract Objects* (Basil Blackwell, Oxford, 1981). **See also** his *Semantic Theory* (Harper and Row, New York, 1972), Chapter I.

22.   **See** C. Peacocke,"Content and Norms in the Natural World", in *Information, Semantics and Epistemology*, ed. by E. Villaneuva (Blackwell, Oxford, 1990).

23.   **See** G.Harman, "Meaning and Semantics", in *Semantics and Philosophy*, ed. by Milton K. Munitz and Peter Unger (New York University Press, New York, 1974), pp. 1-6. **Also see his** "(Non-Solipsist)" Conceptual Role Semantics", in *New Directions in Semantics*, ed. by E. Lepore (Academic Press, London, 1985) pp. 55-81.

24.   **See** Stephen Schiffer,"Does Mentalese have a Compositional Semantics?", in *Meaning in Mind*, ed. by Barry Loewer and Georges Rey (Blackewll, Oxford, 1991).

25.   **See** Jerry A. Fodor, *The Language of Thought* (Harvard University Press, Cambridge, Mass.,1975).

26.   **See** Hans-Georg Gadamer, *Truth and Method*, (Crossroad, New York, 1975), pp. 431-47.

Bibliography

Ammerman, R. (ed.), *Classics of Analytic Philosophy*,Tata McGraw-Hill, New Delhi-Bombay,1965.

Austin, J.L., *How to Do Things with Words*,Clarendon Press, Oxford, 1962.

——, "Performative-Constative", in *The Philosophy of Language*, ed. by J.R. Searle, Oxford University London,1971.

——, "Truth", in *Philosophical Papers*,Oxford University Press, London,1970.

Baker, G. and Hacker, P.M.S., *Frege: Logical Excavations*, Basil Blackwell, Oxford and Oxford University Press, New York, 1984.

Bhartṛhari, *Vākyapadīyam* I, tr. by Satyakama Verma, Munshiram Manoharlal, New Delhi, 1970.

Blackburn, Simon, *Spreading the Word*, Clarendon Press, Oxford, 1984.

Burger, Tyler, "Frege on Truth", *Frege Synthesized*, ed. by Leila Haaparanta and J. Hintikka, D. Reidel, Dordrect, 1986.

Burkhardt, Armin, *Speech Acts, Meaning and Intentions*, de Gruyter, Berlin,1990.

Carnap, Rudolf, *Introduction to Semantics*, Harvard University

Press, Cambridge, Mass.,1942.

——, *Meaning and Necessity: A Study in Semantics and Modal Logic*, 2nd edn., University of Chicago Press, Chicago,1956.

Cassirer, E., *The Philosophy of Symbolic Forms*, Vol. I, tr. by R. Manheim, Yale University Press, New Haven,1955.

Chomsky, Noam, *Aspects of a Theory of Syntax*, MIT Press, Cambridge, Mass., 1965.

——, "Deep Structures, Surface Structures and Semantic Interpretation", in *Semantics: An Interdisciplinary Reader in Philosophy, Linguistics and Psychology*, Cambridge University Press, Cambridge, 1971.

——, *Rules and Representations*, Columbia University Press, New York,1980.

Cohen, Jonathan L., *The Diversity of Meaning*, Methuen and Co., London, 1962.

Davidson, Donald, and Jaakko Hintikka, (eds.), *Words and Objections : Essays on the Work of W.V. Quine*, D.Reidel, Dordrect, 1969.

——, and Harman, (eds.), *Semantics of Natural Language*, D. Reidel, Dordrecht, 1972.

——, *Inquiries into Truth and Interpretation*, Clarendon Press, Oxford,1984.

——, "A Coherence Theory of Truth and Knowledge", in *Truth and Interpretation*, ed. by E. LePore, Basil Blackwell, Oxford,1986.

——, "A Nice Derangement of Epitaphs", in *Truth and Interpretation*, ed. by E. LePore, Basil Blackwell, 1986.

——, "The Structure and Content of Truth", in *Journal of Philosophy*, Vol LXXXVII (1990), pp. 279-328.

Devitt, Michael, *Realism and Truth*, Basil Blackwell, Oxford, 1984.

——, and Sterelny, Kim, *Language and Reality: An Introduction to Philosophy of Language*, Basil Blackwell, Oxford, 1987.

Dewy, John, *Experience and Nature*, Oxford Publishing Company, Calcutta, 1965; Open Court Publishing Company, 1925.

Dummett, Michael, *Frege: Philosophy of Language*, Duckworth, London, 1973; Second edn. 1981.

——, "What is a Theory of Meaning?", in *Mind and Language*, ed. by S. Guttenplan, Clarendon Press, 1975.

——, "What is a Theory of Meaning? II", in *Truth and Meaning: Essays in Semantics*, ed. by Gareth Evans and John McDowell, Clarendon Press, Oxford, 1976.

——, *Elements of Intuitionism*, Clarendon Press, Oxford, 1977.

——, *Truth and Other Enigmas*, Duckworth, London, 1978.

——, *The Interpretation of Frege's Philosophy*, Duckworth, London, 1981.

——, *Frege and Other Philosophers*, Basil Blackwell, Oxford, 1991.

——, *The Logical Basis of Metaphysics*, Harvard University Press, Cambridge, Mass., 1991.

Evans, Gareth, *The Varieties of Reference*, ed. by J. McDowell, Clarendon Press, Oxford and Oxford University Press, New York, 1982.

——, and J. McDowell, (eds.), *Truth and Meaning*, Clarendon Press, Oxford, 1976.

Field, Hartry, "Tarski's Theory of Truth", in *Reference, Truth and Reality*, ed. by Mark Platts, Routledge and Kegan

Paul, London, 1980.

Fodor, Jerry A., *The Language of Thought*, Harvard University Press, Cambridge, Mass., 1975, Paperback.

———, *Representations: Philosophical Essays on the Foundations of Cognitive Science*, Bradford Books/ MIT Press, Cambridge, Mass., 1981.

———, *Psychosemantics*, MIT Press, Cambridge, Mass.,1988.

Frege,Gottlob, *Foundations of Arithmetic*, tr. by J.L. Austin,Basil Blackwell, Oxford, 1950: Reprinted, 1970.

———, *Translations from the Philosophical Writings of Gottlob Frege*, ed. by Peter Geach and Max Black,Oxford, 1952.

———, *The Basic Laws of Arithmetic*, tr.by M. Furth, California University Press, Berkeley and Los Angeles,1964.

———, "The Thought: A Logical Inquiry", in *Philosophical Logic*,ed. by P.F. Strawson, Oxford University Press, London, 1967.

———, *Conceptual Notation*,tr. by T.W. Bynum,Clarendon Press, Oxford, 1972.

———, *Logical Investigations*,ed. by P.T. Geach, Basil Blackwell, Oxford, 1977.

———, *Posthumous Writings*,ed. by H. Hermes et al., Basil Blackwell, Oxford, 1979.

———, *Philosophical and Mathematical Correspondence*,ed. by G. Gabriel, H. Hermes, F. Kambertel, C. Thiel, and A. Veraart, tr. by Haans Kaal, Blackwell, Oxford,1980.

—*Posthumous Writings*, ed. by H. Hermes et al.,Clarendon Press, Oxford, 1981.

French,Peter A. Uehling, T. E. Jr., and Wettstein, Howard K.

(eds.), by *Midwest Studies in Philosophy XII, Realism and Antirealism*, University of Minnesota Press, Minneapolis, 1989.

Gadamer, Hans-Georg, *Truth and Method*, Crossroads, New York, 1975.

Grandy, Richard and Warner, R. (eds.), *Philosophical Grounds of Rationality*, Clarendon Press, Oxford, 1986.

Grice, H.P., "Meaning", in *Philosophical Logic*, ed. by P.F. Strawson, Oxford University Press, Oxford, 1967.

———, "Utterer's meaning, Sentence-meaning and Word-meaning", in *The Philosophy of Language*, ed. by J.R. Searle, Oxford University Press, London, 1971.

Hacking, Ian, "The Paradox of Conversation", in *Truth and Interpretation*, ed. by E. LePore, Basil Blackwell, Oxford, 1989.

Harman, Gilbert, *Thought*, Princeton University Press, Princeton, 1973.

———, "Meaning and Semantics", in *Semantics and Philosophy*, ed. by Milton K. Munitz and Peter Unger, New York University Press, New York, 1974.

———, "(Non-solipsistic) Conceptual Role Semantics", in *New Directions in Semantics*, ed. & tr. by E. LePore, Academic Press, London, 1985.

Hegel, G., *The Phenomenology of Mind*, tr. by J.B. Ballie, Allen and Unwin, London, 1910.

Heidegger, Martin, *Being and Time*, tr. by John Macquarrie and Edward Robinson, Basil Blackwell, Oxford, 1962.

Heijenoort, Van, "Logic as Calculus and Logic as Language", *Synthese* 17 (1967), pp. 324-30.

Hintikka, Merrill, and Hintikka, J., *Investigating Wittgenstein*, Basil Blackwell, Oxford, 1986.

Husserl, Edmund, *Ideas : General Introduction to Pure Phenomenology*, tr. by W.R. Boyce Gibson, George Allen and Unwin, London, 1931.

Kant, Immanuel. *The Critique of Pure Reason*, tr. by Norman Kemp Smith, Mcmillan, London, 1929.

Katz, Jerrold. J., *The Underlying Reality of Language and Its Philosophical Import*, Harper and Row, New York, 1971.

———, *Semantic Theory*, Harper and Row, New York, 1972.

———, *Language and Other Abstract Objects*, Basil Blackwell, Oxford, 1981.

Klemke, E.D., *Essays on Frege*, University of Illinois Press, Urbana, 1968.

Kripke, Saul, "Naming and Necessity", in *Semantics of Natural Languages*, ed. by Donald Davidson and Gilbert Harman, D. Reidel, Dordrecht, 1972.

———, *Naming and Necessity*, Harvard University Press, Cambridge, Mass., 1980.

LePore, E. (ed.), *Truth and Interpretation: Perspectives on the Philosophy of Donald Davidson*, Basil Blackwell, Oxford, 1986.

———, *New Directions in Semantics*, Academic Press, London, 1987.

Lewis, C.I., *Mind and the World Order*, Dover Publications, Inc., New York, 1929.

Lewis, David K., *Conventions: A Philosophical Study*, Harvard University Press, Cambridge, Mass., 1969.

————, *Philosophical Papers*, Vol. I, Oxford University Press, Oxford, 1983.

Linsky, Leonard, *Semantics and Philosophy of Language*, University of Illinois Press, Urbana, 1952.

Loar, Brian, *Mind and Meaning*, Cambridge University Press, Cambridge, 1981.

Lutney, Michael, *Language, Logic and Experience: A Case for Anti-Realism*, Duckworth, London, 1988.

Lycan, W.G., *Logical Form in Natural Language*, Bradford Books/MIT, Cambridge, Mass., 1984.

Malcolm, Norman, *Wittgenstein: Nothing Is Hidden*, Basil Blackwell, Oxford,1986.

McDowell, John, "Truth conditions, Bivalence and Verificationism" in *Meaning and Truth*, ed. by G. Evans, and J. McDowell, Clarendon Press, Oxford, 1976.

————, "On the Sense and Reference of Proper Names", in *Reference, Truth and Reality*, ed. by Mark Platts, Routledge and Kegan Paul, London, 1980.

————, "Anti-Realism and the Epistemology of Understanding", in *Meaning and Understanding*, ed. by Parret, H. and Bouveresse, J., de Gruyter, Berlin, 1981.

McGinn, Colin, *Wittgenstein on Meaning*, Basil Blackwell, Oxford, 1984.

————, "Truth and Use", in *Reference, Truth and Reality*, ed. by Mark Platts, Routledge and Kegan Paul, London,1980.

Mehta, J.L., *The Philosophy of Martin Heidegger*, Banaras Hindu University, Varanasi, 1967.

Millikan, R., *Language, Thought and Other Biological Categories : New Foundations for Realism*, MIT Press,

Canmbridge, Mass., 1984.

Montague, R.E., *Formal Philosophy*, ed. by R.H. Thomason, Yale University Press, New Haven, 1974.

Nagel, Thomas, *The View from Nowhere*, Oxford University Press, New York, 1986.

Parret, H. and Bouveresse, J. (eds.), *Meaning and Understanding*, de Gruyter, Berlin,1981.

Peacocke, Christopher, *Sense and Content*, Clarendon Press, Oxford, 1983.

——, *Thoughts: An Essay on Content*, Basil Blackwell, Oxford, 1986.

——, "Content and Norm in the Natural World", in *Information, Semantics and Epistemology*, ed. by E. Villaneuva, Basil Blackwell, 1990.

Pears, David, "Wittgenstein's Holism", in *Dialectica* 44 (1990), pp. 165-73.

Petit, Philip and McDowell, J. (eds.), *Subject, Thought and Context*, Oxford University Press, Oxford,1986.

Plato, *The Republic*, tr. by Benjamin Jowett, Airmont Publishing Company, Inc., New York, 1968.

Platts, Mark, *The Ways of Meaning*, Routledge and Kegan Paul, London, 1979.

——, *Reference, Truth and Reality: Essays on Philosophy of Language*, Routledge and Kegan Paul, London,1980.

Pradhan, R.C., *Truth, Meaning and Understanding*, Indus Publishing Company, New Delhi,1992.

——, "Wittgenstein on Forms of Life", in *Journal of the Indian Council of Philosophical Research*, Vol.XI, No.3 (1994), pp. 63-79.

Putnam, Hilary, *Mind, Language and Reality, Philosophical Papers Vol. 2*, Cambridge University Press, Cambridge, 1975.

——, *Meaning and the Moral Sciences*, Routledge and Kegan Paul, London, 1978.

——, *Reason, Truth and History*, Cambridge University Press, Cambridge, 1978.

——, *The Many Faces of Realism*, Open Court, La Salle, Illinois, 1991.

Quine, W.V., *Methods of Logic*, Holt, New York, 1959.

——, *Word and Object*, MIT Press, Cambridge, Mass.,1960.

——, *From a Logical Point of View*, 2nd edn., Harvard University Press, Cambridge, Mass., 1961: 1st edn. 1953.

——, *Ontological Relativity and Other Essays*, Columbia University Press, New York, 1969.

——, *Philosophy of Logic*, Prentice-Hall, Englewood Cliffs, N.J., 1970.

——, "Mind and Verbal Dispositions", in *Mind and Language*, ed. by S. Guttenplan, Clarendon Press, Oxford, 1975.

——, *Theories and Things*, Harvard University Press, Cambridge, Mass., 1981.

Ramberg, B.T., *Donald Davidson's Philosophy of Language*, Basil Blackwell, 1989.

Rorty, Richard. *Philosophy and the Mirror of Nature*, Princeton University Press, Princeton, 1973.

——, *Objectivity, Relativism and Truth: Philosophical Papers* Vol. I, Cambridge University Press, Cambridge, 1991.

————, *Essays on Heidegger and Others: Philosophical Papers* Vol. 2, Cambridge University Press, Cambridge, 1991.

Rosenberg, Jay F., *Linguistic Representation*, D. Reidel, Dordrecht, 1974.

Russell, Bertrand., *Introduction to Mathematical Philosophy*, Allen and Unwin, London, 1919.

Schiffer, Stephen, *Meaning*, Clarendon Press, Oxford, 1972.

————, "Does Mentalese Have a Comositional Semantics?", in *Meaning in Mind, Fodor and His Critics*, ed. by Barry Loewer and George Rey, Basil Blackwell, Oxford, 1991.

Searle, John R., *Speech Acts: An Essay in Philosophy of Language*, Cambridge University Press, Cambridge, 1969.

————, *Intentionality*, Cambridge University Press, Cambridge, 1983.

————, (ed.), *The Philosophy of Language*, Oxford University Press, London, 1971.

Sen, P.K., *Reference and Truth*, ICPR and Allied Publishers, New Delhi, 1991.

Strawson, P.F., "On Referring", in *Classics of Analytic Philosophy*, ed. by R. Ammerman, Tata McGraw-Hill Publishing Company Ltd., New Delhi-Bombay, 1965.

————, (ed.) *Philosophical Logic*, Oxford University Press, London, 1967.

————, "Intention and Convention in Speech Acts", in *The Philosophy of Language*, ed. by J.R. Searle, Cambridge University Press, Cambridge, 1971.

————, *Logico-Linguistic Papers*, Methuen and Co., London, 1972.

Steiner, George. *Heidegger,* Fontana Press, London, 1978.

Tarski, Alfred, *Logic, Semantics, Metamathematics,* tr. by J.H. Woodger, Clarendon Press, 1956.

Taylor, Barry., (ed.), *Michael Dummett : Contribution to Philosophy,* Martinus Nijhoff, The Hague, 1987.

Wittgenstein, Ludwig, *Philosophical Investigations,* tr. by Anscombe, Basil Blackwell, Oxford, 1953.

———, *Tractatus Logico-Philosophicus,* tr. by D .F. Pears and B.F. McGuinness, Routledge and Kegan Paul, London, 1961.

———, *Notebooks* 1914-16, tr. by G.E.M. Anscombe, Basil Blackwell, 1961.

———, *Zettel,* tr. by G.E.M. Anscombe, Basil Blacwell, Oxford, 1967.

Wright, Crispin, *Wittgenstein on the Foundations of Mathematics,* Duckworth, London, 1981.

———, *Realism, Meaning and Truth,* Basil Blackwell, Oxford, 1986.

———, (ed.), *Frege, Tradition and Influence,* Basil Blackwell, Oxford, 1984.

Ziff, Paul, *Semantic Analysis,* Cornell University Press, Ithaca, N.Y., 1960.

Index